On Being A
TEACHER

Nathalie J. Gehrke

Teachers talk about teachings. Real teachers study their pupils as well. Most of all, teachers should be studied.
Musa Kazim

Library of Congress Cataloging in Publication Data

Gehrke, Nathalie J. (Nathalie Jean), 1945-
   On being a teacher/Nathalie J. Gehrke.
      p.   cm.
   Bibliography: p.
   1. Teaching I. Title.
LB1025.2.G424 1987   371.1'02—dc19   8-
7-26141
ISBN 0-912099-03-8 : $12.50

Published by Kappa Delta Pi
An International Honor Society in Education
P.O. Box A
West Lafayette, Indiana 47906

The purpose of Kappa Delta Pi is to recognize
outstanding contributions to education. To this
end it invites to membership such persons who
exhibit commendable personal qualities, worthy
educational ideals, and sound scholarship, without regard to race, color, religion, or sex.

Contents

To my first grade teacher, Mrs. Victoria Kamke, and to my geometry and Latin teacher, Mrs. Joyce Kilmer. How fortunate I am that they both chose to teach.

Message from the President

Kappa Delta Pi is an honor society of, about, and for teachers. Our society programs are designed to recognize and honor excellence in scholarship and professional contributions; to provide opportunities for professional development; to give all teachers (those yet to be, new, experienced, and retired) a forum to share ideas and concerns. In keeping with the philosophy of our society programs, this book, *On Being A Teacher*, was written by Nathalie Gehrke to help us examine who we are, where we are going, what happens when we get there, and our decisions to leave. Her analysis of the process of "Choosing," "Learning," "Beginning," "Continuing," and "Leaving" the profession is thorough and thought provoking.

As I read her words, I found myself reflecting upon my own beliefs and attitudes about teaching and re-examining my decision to become a teacher. I was, according to Gehrke, one of those who chose early. As long as I can remember, I wanted to be a teacher; somewhere during junior high school I decided to teach mathematics, because it was easy and fun and I helped my class-mates with their homework. Teaching seemed to be right; after all, it provided a brush with immortality ("stake in the future"). Just think of how many lives a teacher can influence over a twenty or thirty year career. A teacher makes a mark on the world which only a few may see, but from which many will profit. A teacher can change the "course of human events" (crusader) but may never really know when or to what extent. All these aspects of teaching are explained and described in the book in ways I had not thought about in over twenty years. The catharsis was good for me, particularly since I am now a teacher educator and part of my responsibility lies in helping people become teachers. I must deal with students whose reasons for choosing teaching as a career often are not as esoteric as mine, but yet are certainly legitimate and realistic.

In the remaining sections of the book, Nathalie Gehrke discusses teaching as a learning process, including credentialing practices and teacher education reforms. She uses anecdotes to highlight the "ups and downs" of a beginning teacher, and she reminds those of us who now work with beginning teachers of what it was like to be the "new teacher on the block."

The section of the book devoted to "Continuing" puts into perspective the problems and frustrations of being a teacher. No one can deny they exist, but through Gehrke's analysis they seem understandable and even manageable.

I was most intrigued by the ideas presented in the section entitled "Leaving." Perhaps this affected me so because I have contemplated leaving when pressures, rules, regulations, and negative attitudes toward the profession seemed insurmountable. On the other hand, many of my friends and colleagues are or are thinking about retiring. Some have opted for early retirement, tired and frustrated. Others are ending their careers as they began, enthusiastic and optimistic. What makes the difference?

On Being a Teacher is excellent reading, no matter where you are in your career as a teacher. If you are "beginning," you will get some excellent insights into what to expect as you progress through your career. If you are at the middle career stage, you can benefit from a re-examination of why you are here and what lies ahead. If you have retired or left the profession for other reasons, you may reflect upon your decision and reinforce or find some satisfaction with that decision.

President John F. Kennedy said in his message to Congress on January 11, 1962, "a child miseducated is a child lost." Individuals who become teachers and fail to realize the importance of their roles and duties as teachers can easily miseducate masses of children. We don't want that to happen in our country where "the schools are the cradle of democracy" (William O. Douglass, 1952) and the teachers have the freedom to shape the attitudes and beliefs of young minds toward the society in which they live.

Teaching is this country's most honorable profession and those of us who have made the choice to teach must never forget the awesomeness and the responsibility of our choice. For it is through us that we will protect our democracy and our freedom.

Marcella L. Kysilka
President, Kappa Delta Pi
1986-1988

Acknowledgements

I'd like to thank the many teachers who have talked with me over the past twelve years about their life and work. Learners, beginners, and experienced teachers, all spoke willingly. Each added to my understanding, and I hope I have transmitted their words with accuracy and care. Thanks also to Rosemary Sheffield and Andrea Marrett, each of whom has read and offered helpful comments on chapters of the book, and to Harold Shane, who commented on the early outlined proposal. Thanks to Gerald Ponder, the Kappa Delta Pi monograph series editor, who often has made my thoughts appear clearer by the skill of his editorial pen. More important, he believed this book was possible, even when I doubted. Finally, thanks to my husband, Ed, and son, Adam, who not only have been supportive, but somehow have tolerated and avoided tripping over my stacks of research materials spread throughout the house.

N.J.G.

We wish to thank the following for granting permission to reprint the passages quoted in the epigraphs: From *Teacher in America* by Jacques Barzun, copyright 1951 by Jacques Barzun, by permission of Little, Brown and Company (Foreword: Chapters 1, 3, and 4); E. P. Dutton & Co., Inc., *The Way of the Sufi* by Idries Shah, 1970 (Title page); The Delta Kappa Gamma Society *Bulletin*, "Epitaph for an Educator" by Elsie Evans, Index 1985 (Epilogue); *English Journal*, "Milton and I: Teaching English in paradise re-lost" by G. H. Henry, 64(2), (Chapter 5); and Alfred A. Knopf, Inc., *The Art of Teaching* by Gilbert Highet, 1958 (Chapter 2).

FOREWORD

There was a time when Mr. Einstein was not quite sure what eight times nine came to. He had to learn, and to learn he had to be taught. The reason teaching has to go on is that children are not born human; they are made so.

Jacques Barzun
Teacher in America

This book is about teaching. It considers teaching as a lifelong process, as a worthy career, as a reflective profession, and as becoming more fully human. It was written to synthesize what we know about teaching as a way of work and a way of life and to present that knowledge in a way that will be helpful to people entering teaching, teachers who are reflecting on their own work, and the teacher educators and supervisors who work with them all.

The bent to teach exists in all of us. It is absolutely necessary to the life of the species. Becoming a better teacher thus can mean growing to be more fully human. While we each learn from interacting with our environment, there are some things that we learn only through the mediation of other people. Teachers persuade us of the need to learn, focus our attention on what must be learned, model critical behavior, enhance aspects of learning tasks or segment them to make them more learnable, give us opportunities to practice, encourage, reward or punish us for our performances. Without this mediation we may continue to function, but we will lack some of the most powerful knowledge that makes a full life possible. The Israeli educator Reuven Feuerstein has held that mediation is most important when learning the ideas, ways of thinking, and attitudes which help us manage our lives and live harmoniously in our world.

Because mediation is crucial for the lives of all human beings, teaching is a worthy career. Its *value*, like its rewards, can be calculated in money, power, or prestige. Such calculations will be disappointing. However, its *worth* in enhancing the quality of life is inestimable. Complaining about teachers, schools, and education in general always has been a popular pastime. But when men and women are pressed to name the few most significant persons in their lives, they name teachers again and again. In what other career would this occur so regularly?

The ability to teach at least a little is, then, something we all hold in common. But the conscious effort toward perfecting that ability is what distinguishes professional teachers from others. The point at which one moves from following a tendency to the thoughtful behavior which we expect of professional teachers is uncertain. But development beyond that point is the goal of teacher education and staff development programs.

The ultimate responsibility for continued growth lies with the individual teacher, of course, and I believe it is a *lifelong* responsibility. The process of growing includes constant self-examination, reflection, and change at all stages. Teachers who do not engage in this self-examination, reflection, and change may be considered amateurs only, even if they "teach" for thirty years. They are, to use Jacques Barzun's words, "merely connected with education," not teachers. Becoming a better teacher means becoming a better learner.

I believe that people do want to grow and become better. And they want to become better teachers. They engage in what O. G. Brim calls "self-socialization," putting themselves in situations where others will help shape them in becoming what they themselves want to become.

Through the chapters that follow I examine five phases of becoming and living as a teacher from an interactive, self-socialization perspective. The first chapter examines the different reasons or motivators for choosing teaching. It focuses on who chooses teaching and when, and on what and who influence that choice. The second chapter explains what we know about learning to be a teacher. It looks at learning both the craft of teaching and the role of teacher

In the third chapter the situations faced by beginning teachers are described along with their responses to them. It is a chapter filled with the problems encountered, certainly. But it is filled too with the joys of success. The fourth chapter looks at continuing teachers' development. It describes the changes teachers go through over the years, their efforts at renewing enthusiasm, balancing their personal and occupational roles, and continuing development as human beings and professionals. The fifth chapter completes the whole with a look at closing a teaching career. It describes both voluntary and forced early leaving as well as the movement toward retirement of the experienced veteran. Each kind of leaving has special characteristics and different consequences for the teachers and their students during the period of leaving.

Throughout the whole I have tried to create a portrait of teaching as a career that is both honest and kind. Honest, in being based on a careful review of the study of teaching. Kind, in describing it from the perspective of one who has found a good measure of happiness as a teacher, teacher of teachers, and student of teaching for nearly all of my adult life. If I sometimes seem more kind than honest, I hope to be indulged. If I sometimes appear more honest than kind, I hope to be understood.

N.J.G.
Seattle
1987

1 CHOOSING

... I conclude that the teaching impulse goes something like this: a fellow human being is puzzled or stymied. He wants to open a door or spell "accommodate." The would-be helper has two choices. He can open the door, spell the word; or he can show his pupil how to do it for himself. The second way is harder and takes more time, but a strong instinct in the born teacher makes him prefer it. It seems somehow to turn an accident into an opportunity for permanent creation.

Jacques Barzun
Teacher in America

We all make choices that send us down a life path that is at the same time universal and unique. Through each choice, we join others who have made that same choice. But through our individual decision patterns and the meanings we give to those decisions we distinguish ourselves from others. Among life's most important decisions is the choice that sends us into an occupation. Our choice of work shapes whom we meet, who will become our colleagues, our friends, our adversaries — sometimes even our husbands or wives. It can influence our health, our values, our leisure, and our politics; certainly it influences how we see ourselves.

Choosing to be a teacher links us to all other teachers, past and present. What kinds of people are teachers? Why did they choose teaching rather than another occupation? Are the people who choose teaching today different from those who chose it in the past? Knowing the answers to these questions can help those who choose to teach better understand themselves and their decisions.

Timing: When Do You Know?

When do you first know that you should become a teacher — know that teaching is right for you and you are right for teaching? What are the reasons for your choice? Some teachers say that they *always* knew that teaching was the career for them. Some decided during late adolescence or early adulthood. Others say they had to live a bit and experience other things before they could see that teaching was where they belonged, so they worked at other careers first. Each of us has a unique story, but there are some patterns to the timing of the decision to teach, and that timing is related both to the reasons we give for choosing teaching and the image we wish to project as a teacher.

When elementary school teachers are asked when they decided to become teachers, they commonly report that they made their decisions as young children. They say things like:

> [I thought about teaching] *ever since I can remember, but definitely by sixth grade.*
> or:
> *I thought about being a teacher when I was eight or nine years old . . . I want to be a teacher because I love interacting with a group of people I can relate to every day . . .*

These are the teachers who reminisce about playing school or about "being the teacher" to brothers and sisters or playmates. Others see these people as teachers, and they accept that vision for themselves.

Junior high and high school teachers, on the other hand, usually make the decision to teach at a later stage in life. Some decide as adolescents, others as young adults.

> *Early inclinations [to teach] came first in my high school years when I had an excellent biology teacher and excellent coaches. I loved science then and even more in college. I also had success in helping fellow students with science and knew I could not only successfully teach science professionally, but could do it and enjoy it very much.*

Benjamin Wright reported finding differences in decision points between elementary and secondary teachers in 1968, as did Dan Lortie in 1975. The prospective teachers quoted above were speaking in 1985. This long-standing difference between elementary and secondary teachers can be explained at least in part by a commonsense notion that people can't identify with a particular role until they have seen it. Thus future elementary teachers begin to identify with their own elementary teachers well before future junior high and high school teachers can begin to identify with comparable role models. Identifying with same-sex roles models —girls with women and boys with men—is very common, so because most elementary teachers are women, this early role identification may be less likely for boys. They begin to find significant numbers of potential male role models only in secondary schools. Not surprisingly, they are more likely to become junior high and high school teachers themselves.

Not all elementary, and certainly not all secondary teachers make decisions to become teachers before they enter college. Many do not decide that they will until they are in their junior or senior years; some decide well after graduation. This opportunity to delay entry into teaching as a career is not common to many professional occupations. But because the broad category of "teacher" includes art teachers as well as business teachers, physical education teachers as well as chemistry teachers, and English teachers as well as mathematics teachers, it excludes very few college majors. Further, the historic demand for relatively large numbers of teachers and the short preparation period make it feasible for persons to choose teaching on short notice and to be reasonably sure that they can find jobs after they complete their coursework.

In *Schoolteacher*, Lortie described this "wide decision-range" for entry into teaching as a facilitator in the development of the large pool of teachers needed. He also proposed that those who choose early in the range are more likely to talk about their work in glowing, emotional terms, while those who choose later are more apt to describe it as a pragmatic decision. Those deciding early speak of teaching as a calling; those deciding later, of the "convertability of prior education." Consider, for example, these two comments about reasons for choosing teaching:

> *I enjoy seeing people get excited about [learning]. I'm very excited about my [teaching] and I feel others get excited about it when they're around me. I also look forward to creating and implementing my own ideas for effective learning.*

or:

[I chose teaching because] it is honorable work with a favorable combination of income and leave time.

Using Lortie's propositions, distinguishing the early from the late decider should be easy.

Carolyn Bogad discovered five categories of student teachers, based on their primary reasons for choosing teaching. Her study linked recruitment motivation to learning patterns in teacher education programs and to later teaching behavior. Bogad interviewed 55 prospective secondary teachers, then observed fifteen of them throughout their credential program year. She became a non-participant observer at all formal and informal events held as part of that year's credential program. She found one group of individuals for whom there was a sense of "occupational fit," much like that described by the early deciders. The four other primary categories included what I will label *the crusaders, the content specialists, the converts* and *the freefloaters.*

Crusaders are those who decide to enter teaching in order to change the system or change society. They have seen a wrong — sometimes bad teaching, sometimes an unjust situation for young people — and they believe they can "make a difference." The percentage of those who enter teaching for this reason varies in proportion to the degree of idealistic activism found in the larger society at the time. Many crusaders entered teaching in the late sixties and early seventies when critical issues such as the Vietnam war and civil rights dominated the political and social scene. Today's crusaders may be environmentalists or proponents of nuclear disarmament. Tomorrow, there will be new issues.

Content Specialists are those who decide on teaching primarily as a way to continue to be involved with the subject matter in which they have majored. Some of these specialists see few choices but teaching. As one of Bogad's prospective teachers explained:

If you are a history major you can be a lawyer or a teacher. I didn't want to be a lawyer.

Others see teaching their content as a *very* positive choice among alternatives.

[I chose teaching because I'd be] working in my field which is also my hobby, [and because I'd be] turning students on to biology and the life science and environment around them.

Converts are those who have entered other careers, only to find that teaching is what they really would like to do. Those who return to follow "the road not taken" generally are several years older than their classmates. They often have been quite successful in their previous careers, but are likely to report that they hadn't felt that the work had let them "help someone" or live out their own commitments to lifelong learning. One 37-year old history major wrote:

> *After 15 years of working in scientific research for the government, I decided that I wanted more contact with the "real world." I also wished to work with young people in a multi-cultural, multi-ethnic environment.*

This group includes former housewives, ministers and priests, persons from business and industry, and even a number of retired military officers.

A fourth group of late deciders, the *freefloaters*, are not deciders at all, but persons who hope that teaching, or at least teacher preparation, will help them decide what to do with their lives. Bogad reported that while observing student teachers whom she later classified in this group she saw:

> *. . . one student in a junior high classroom attempt to give a lecture while dressed in shorts and beach thongs, one student sitting in an assigned seat with the students who raised her hand to ask if she 'could teach now?', and one student who showed up fifteen minutes late to his class because he 'couldn't find a projector in the school'.*

These students had had little or no work experience, minimal experience with children or youth, and often remembered junior high and high school as painful times. They were likely not to complete a teacher education program or, if they did, not to pursue a teaching job.

Because of the traditionally open access to teacher preparation programs, these unfocused people have had little difficulty entering programs in the past. As screening procedures are tightened, fewer freefloaters will be found among their more mature classmates. Some will finish and obtain positions, however, and we will see them again among the beginning teachers.

Motivations: Why Teachers Decide to Teach

Suggesting that people chose to become teachers for a single identifiable reason is dangerous. People are too complex for such absolutes. However, each time researchers have sought to identify the major motivations to teach and the satisfiers in teaching, they have concluded that the most powerful reason is the desire to work with or help other people. A 1985 study by Sandra Roberson, Timothy Keith and Ellis Page used information on over 10,000 high school seniors gathered in the National High School and Beyond study in 1980. They confirmed that of those seniors, the 688 who aspired to teaching rated a good income, success and security well below working with friendly people and doing important or interesting work. These quotations illustrate this pattern.

> I had very good experiences in my elementary and high school years and I wish to pass on such good learning experiences.

> I want to have a positive effect on the world . . . I'd like to work with people of similar interests and motivations—teachers rarely list money and "getting to the top" as their primary motivation.

In their book, *Teachers, Their World, and Their Work*, Ann Lieberman and Lynn Miller see in these kinds of remarks evidence of teachers' desires for "a stake in the future." This stake is sought not through giving the gift of biological life, like parenting, but through the gift of knowledge — the life of the mind. This is the important work that ranks high on the list of motivators identified by aspiring teachers in the High School and Beyond study. It also relates to the "service" and "continuation" themes identified by Lortie. Service is, of course, related to the helping of others, while continuation refers to motives to stay in an environment one enjoys, doing the kinds of activities one has enjoyed doing. Those who choose to teach because of their own joy in learning and their wish to share it demonstrate both motivational themes.

Becoming a teacher often is explained as responding to a call. This "call" appears linked to the desire to help people. People are "called" to be ministers, doctors, nurses, social workers, counselors, or teachers. But one does not hear of "being called" to be a supermarket manager or a secretary, an executive or a plumber. Of course, not all teachers (and not all other social service workers) describe this calling. To some, work is work. They may choose teaching simply because it is convenient, provides a job, or is all that seems available at the time. Teaching may be basically "honorable work with a favorable combination of income and leave time." One prospective teacher, when asked why he had chosen teaching, responded simply, "employment."

Are teachers who feel "called" better teachers than those who have chosen for other reasons? We don't know. There is, however, evidence that people who choose teaching simply because they don't know what to do with their lives (the freefloaters) are more likely to have problems. There does seem to be a link between the sense of being called and what we often term commitment—a characteristic that many place at the top of their list of attributes of a good teacher. But commitment is something which can and often does change on the job; you need not necessarily have "it" complete when you walk in the school door, nor can we be assured that once you have "it" it will always be there.

There also are secondary attractors to teaching which appear on lists of reasons for choosing teaching, but are rarely identified as the primary or major motivators. Such things as *time compatibility* appear here. That they can teach, yet be home when their own children get home is seen as a great bonus by many women (and some men) with families. That teachers can spend the summer months with their children, or pursuing hobbies, second jobs, or further education is an additional bonus.

The *portability* of the occupation is another attractor. No matter where one might move, teachers will always be needed. As one aspiring teacher said:

> It will prove to be a useful skill when I move to Japan
> with my husband, and it will provide a skill that will
> help me to travel anywhere in the world.

The ability to move in and out of teaching is yet one more attractor, especially to women who wish to combine a career and parenting. Teaching skills are not likely to become obsolete during one's absences from the field. A return after dropping out for awhile may require some updating, but is not unusually difficult. Perhaps "bonus" is a good way to look at these elements through the eyes of beginners. Later in teachers' careers they may come to take on greater significance, but at the beginning they are more icing than cake.

Influences: Teachers as Guides and Role Models

What part do others play in our decisions to enter teaching? A large part. There is overwhelming evidence that teachers themselves are highly influential in the career choices of future teachers. That does not mean they consciously try to persuade others. Rather, they affect the choice by their presence, by their example, and perhaps by their subtle suggestions. Teachers and those who aspire to teach, no matter what their gender, content area, or grade level, report that former teachers have been significant in their decisions to teach. This was particularly well-substantiated by the recent analysis of the High School and Beyond data mentioned earlier, and can be illustrated by these remarks:

> I thought about [teaching] when I was young—every time I had a good teacher. I enjoy teaching. It seems to be what I'm always asked to do. . .

Prospective teachers may consider the love, respect and admiration engendered by remembered teachers as the feelings they wish to inspire among others. It may be a simple step from that recognition to the choice of teaching as an occupation.

We should not be surprised that today many are concerned about the low morale of teachers. If one generation's teachers include many who regret their choices, they are not only less likely to be good teachers, they also are more likely to signal their dissatisfaction to the potential teachers among their students. Many fine teachers of the future could be lost. One woman, beginning a teacher preparation program at the age of 37, was nearly lost this way:

> Teaching was my ambition until 1977 when I observed the difficulties inherent in the system and decided against it. I observed some very bitter, disillusioned teachers and I feared I might go their route into cynicism. (Since then I have developed "flexibility.")

Though teachers are highly influential in the career decisions of many aspiring teachers, they are not the only people with influence. Parents, too, have an effect. We have long recognized that teachers beget teachers — that teaching runs in families. To be sure, Lortie has pointed out that teaching is such a massive occupation, with such historically high turnover, that the possibility that a family member has been a teacher is very great for most people. But the attitudes and values of family members who are or have been teachers are transmitted and reinforced in such ways that choosing to teach seems natural, uncoerced, and right. Even among families with no current or former teachers, an orientation toward the kinds of values embodied in teaching subtly shapes career choice. The belief that good work is work in which we help others, regardless of money, is transmitted by many families, particularly to daughters.

Parents influence their children's choices to become teachers in other, less direct ways too. Studies of the relationships of women teachers and their parents done by Benjamin Wright and Shirley Tuska indicate that different patterns in those relationships are related to choices to teach at different levels in the school. For example, women who reported very warm, loving relationships with their mothers were more likely to be elementary teachers, while women who had pleasant but not close relationships with their mothers and rather cool distant relationships with their fathers were more likely to be high school teachers. Some have speculated that the power of parents to instill the use of certain models of teaching has made those models so long a part of our very personalities that they are almost impossible to change. If we gravitate toward a level of school where we feel at home, the forces shaping our particular choices about teaching may have been at work long before we could even talk.

Characteristics: What Kinds of People Choose Teaching?

In looking at when, why, and how people choose teaching, we also have begun to describe the people who choose to be teachers. We know that they are people who felt an occupational fit at an early age, or who became crusaders, or subject matter specialists, or late converts. We know they are persons who enjoy helping others and like the school environment. And we know that they are people who have had at least one good teacher role model and parents who were teachers or who highly valued teaching. But recently much attention has focused on other characteristics of those choosing teaching. Policy makers and the public are concerned that the quality of new teachers has decreased as highly capable women and members of minority groups turned to other more lucrative careers in business and industry.

What do we know that may help provide perspective on this issue? Several things. We know that today, as for over a century, women are more likely to choose to be teachers than are men. In the study by Roberson, Keith, and Page, the best predictor of those seniors who planned to enter teaching was gender. From that study, we know, too, that the relative percentage of minorities planning to enter teaching is somewhat lower than the percentage of whites. Based on the same study and on the work of Lortie, we know that women who choose teaching come from many different socio-economic levels, while men who become teachers are more likely to come from lower and middle socio-economic levels. Finally, from the work of Phillip Schlechty and Victor Vance we know that women entering teaching generally have scored higher on measures of ability than have men.

According to Lortie and to Roberson, Keith, and Page, those who plan to teach and those who actually become teachers have been and still are likely to be family-oriented and to be relatively religious. In addition, they are fairly conservative in their political beliefs. Except perhaps for the crusaders, they generally are satisfied with the social, political, and educational systems in which they find themselves. That does not mean that they have no complaints or interests in change. But they basically believe that the current systems are sound and any changes they deem important are possible within them.

What then of the declining capability issue? There is conflicting evidence on the degree to which young people with higher achievement test scores and higher grade point averages have, over the past few years, begun to choose other occupations. Studies based on SAT scores of high school seniors done by Vance and Schlechty and on ACT scores done by Weaver seem to show that capable students are less likely to choose teaching. But a more recent reanalysis of the same data from the National Longitudinal Survey of the high school class of 1972 done by F. Howard Nelson showed that those who became teachers compared favorably with other college graduates on such measures as the SAT, ACT, and high school class rank when the data were weighted appropriately. Nelson's study also demonstrated that less than 25 percent of those who became teachers had planned to major in education as high school seniors, so that he cautioned against public policy "fallaciously guided by widely cited research based only on the study of prospective education majors among college-bound seniors."

The capability of those entering teaching is less in doubt than had been feared. Still there is continuing support for the proposition that the more capable are likely to leave teaching prematurely, though Nelson's work shows this to be much more of a problem in non-public schools than in public schools. Teaching will never be highly paid work, and it probably will never be among the occupations with the highest status. The sheer number of teachers needed for the schools and the fact that public monies are used to support them will continue to moderate any pay increases. Those factors also militate against any great changes in teachers' social status. Among those for whom income and status are important, then, teaching will continue to be less attractive. If social trends continue to place greater emphasis on income and status, then the occupation of teaching is likely to lose more potential candidates, though not necessarily the more capable.

The teaching occupation will depend in the future on potential teachers seeking the kinds of rewards that have always drawn people to teaching: helping others, making a difference in someone's life, sharing one's own excitement about the subject matter. We must hope that in that group will be as many able people as possible. We must do what we can to see that that is so. But more, we must seek to develop a working environment which keeps good teachers in teaching, which promotes growth toward excellence and personal fulfillment. Sarah Lawrence Lightfoot put it well when she said,

> In order to achieve goodness . . . schools must collect
> good teachers and treat them like chosen people.

We must treat teachers well because those who choose to teach do not choose to do so once and for all. They choose teaching one year at a time. Unlike many occupations which are seamless in nature, teaching is interrupted by the extended summer break, which provides a natural point of departure. It is further punctuated each year by signing a new, one-year contract. The explicit nature of this annual commitment to teach seems more likely to stimulate a reassessment of past choice than might occur in those occupations where one year just runs into the next. Leaving is thus made easier for teachers than for others. For good teachers to stay, they must find strong reasons to commit for one more year—to choose again to teach.

The choice to teach is an active, yet influenced choice for beginners and veterans alike. We each, in our paths to teaching, are shaped by our environment, but we also shape it and construct its meaning, giving our unique reasons for the choices. That is why, as we choose, learn, and then become teachers, we can become more like each other and yet more unique.

Selected References

Barzun, J. *Teacher in America.* Boston: Little, Brown & Co., 1945.

Bogad, C. M. Recruitment and Socialization as Recurring Issues in Teacher Education. A paper presented at the annual meeting of the American Educational Research Association. New Orleans. 1984.

Lieberman, A., and L. Miller. *Teachers, Their World and Their Work: Implications for School Improvement.* Alexandria, VA: Association for Supervision & Curriculum Development, 1984.

Lightfoot, S. L. *The Good High School: Portraits of Character and Culture.* New York: Basic Books, 1983.

Lortie, D. *Schoolteacher: A Sociological Study.* Chicago: University of Chicago Press, 1975.

Nelson, F. H. New Perspectives on the Teacher Quality Debate: Empirical Evidence from the National Longitudinal Survey. *Journal of Educational Research.* Vol. 78 (3) Jan.-Feb., 1985. 133-140.

Roberson, S. D., T. Z. Keith, & E. B. Page. Now Who Aspires to Teach? *Educational Researcher.* 12, (6) 1983. 13-20.

Vance, V. A. & P. C. Schlechty. The Distribution of Academic Ability in the Teaching Force: Policy Implications. *Phi Delta Kappan.* 63 (1) 1982. 22-27.

Weaver, W. T. Educators in Supply and Demand: Effects on Quality. *School Review.* 86 (4) 1978. 552-593.

Wright, B. & S. A. Tuska. *Student and First Year Teachers' Attitudes Toward Self and Others.* Chicago: University of Chicago and the Office of Education, U.S.H.E.W., 1966.

_____. From Dream to Life in the Psychology of Becoming a Teacher *School Review.* 76 September, 1968. 253-293.

2 LEARNING

Therefore teaching is inseparable from learning. Every good teacher will learn more about his subject every year — every month, every week if possible.

Gilbert Highet
The Art of Teaching

O thers may teach us instructional skills, but we teach ourselves to be teachers. We *create* ourselves as teachers. No two students will ever experience a teacher education program quite the same way; no two will become mirror images. Still, the experiences of one may illuminate the experiences of many, so in the next few pages we will follow one fictitious student while she moves through a teacher education program. In so doing, we can consider the learning of skills and the learning of role. We can look at the current status of teacher education programs and at emerging trends. The questions to be answered in all of this are, "What kind of experience can students expect when they enter a teacher education program in the near future? What kinds of changes can they expect in themselves?"

Before we meet our student teacher I'd like to make known my assumptions about how we learn to teach and review a bit of teacher education history. The statement of my assumptions should remind you (and me) that this is still just one person's point of view, while the history may give some perspective on today's programs.

In a formal teacher education program students focus directly on learning to be a teacher, on creating self as teacher. But learning to teach begins as early as we learn to be human beings. We learn from watching others, from being taught, from trying to teach. We learn to teach as we were taught — by parents, sisters and brothers, the adults in the circle around us, from television and film characters, news reporters and Mr. Rogers. Some elements of our teaching, such as our uses of rewards and punishments, criticism and praise, can be traced to early experiences with primary caregivers, but much of this behavior is modified by powerful experiences with those significant teachers we all remember. Dan Lortie pointed out that we each spend thousands of hours with school teachers before we ever enter teacher education programs — a long time to absorb their patterns of behavior, albeit from the naive perspective of the student.

Because of all this prior learning, we may think of a formal program of teacher education not as teaching totally new skills in the way that one is taught how to type or how to apply a tourniquet. Formal programs rather teach guiding principles and terminology for actions, concepts and patterns, many of which we already *know* tacitly. They offer opportunities to practice and perfect skills, teach processes of reflection and problem solving. They also socialize prospective teachers to the role of teacher.

Sometimes a teacher education program runs counter to an individual's role personalization efforts. That is, the content and experiences in the teacher education program conflict with a prospective teacher's efforts to shape the teacher role to meet personal needs for respect, liking, belonging, and a sense of competence. Each candidate may be required to demonstrate the same proficiency in instructional skills, but each will negotiate differently between personal needs and the socializing press of teacher educators, practicing teachers and administrators, parents, and students. Student teachers, each working from a personal image of the ideal teacher, selectively pick up cues from these sources about desirable teacher behaviors. Each creates a unique teacher-self, tempered by the influences of others, but still a creative product unlike any other.

In the earliest years of this country, no special preparation was required of any aspiring teacher candidates, according to Willard Elsbree; neither socialization to the role nor training in the skills was formalized. While some teachers had received an education beyond the secondary school, many rural teachers were educated only through the level they were about to teach. Colleges were not open to women and because of this women could rarely qualify to teach above the elementary level.

Before the nineteenth century women teachers were outnumbered by men, but women began to enter the profession in large numbers about the same time that teacher preparation programs were first offered in the mid-1830's. Such programs were generally about a year in length and included studies and practica similar to those found today. Of course, these early programs could be entered after only two years of high school — considerably less than the prerequisites students must complete today, and far less than the requirement of a completed bachelor's degree being advocated by some teacher educators.

Jean

Jean, our student teacher, is twenty-one, single, and white. Her mother, a practical nurse, and her father, an insurance salesman, have worked hard to put Jean and her brother through college. Jean has had to work summers as a camp counselor and weekend jobs as a waitress to help out. She is one of the crusaders, and has chosen teaching not only because she likes working with youth, but also as a way to influence society's apparent indifference to the abuse of the environment. An outdoor enthusiast and activist in Greenpeace, Jean nearly had completed a university degree in Biology when she decided that the best route to her goal of protecting the environment was by reaching young people. Remembering how she was first aroused to interest in science by her seventh grade teacher, Jean decided to apply for entrance to a program to prepare junior high-middle school teachers.

Entering the Program

When Jean seeks to enter the teacher education program at her university, she is surprised to learn how selective the program is. She must take a standardized achievement test to verify her general academic competence. She must have the approval of the department in which she is completing her major. She must have a strong cumulative grade point average. These requirements must be met before she is even placed in a pool of eligible students. Then she must successfully complete an interview with a committee composed of university education faculty members and public school teachers and administrators.

Jean passes through the tests and screenings with considerable aplomb, though the interview makes her especially nervous. She is delighted and relieved to get word that she has finally been accepted to begin during the next term. She is among the lucky ones, she thinks. But she is unaware of any controversy about the process she has gone through. Some say that screening like Jean experienced by public school personnel is harmful because those doing the screening will choose only candidates who are similar to themselves in philosophy, political views and personality characteristics. Others say that only through such screening will educators gain control of their profession and quality be assured. These arguments about replication and about who should control the profession surface at many points as teachers move along their career paths, but formal teacher education programs are likely to be the major skirmish zone because they serve as gatekeepers to the profession.

Jean's admissions experience may have been more demanding than typical programs across the country, but the past five years have brought significant voluntary and state-mandated movement in this direction. Easy entrance to teacher education programs and to the teaching profession may well be a thing of the past. Colleges may have to be restrictive in admissions or lose the right to offer programs if their graduates do poorly on state teacher examinations, mandates for which have increased dramatically in recent years. In 1981, for example, fifteen states required some form of examination to measure general academic competence, subject matter and/or teaching competence. By 1986, 21 states required students to pass a test before entering a teacher education program, and by 1988, at least thirty-two states will require testing at some point before certification.

Beginning a Program

Jean now begins her first term in the education program with twice-weekly observations in a middle school (grades 6-8) at some distance from the campus, catch-up coursework in science fields outside Biology to fulfill her certification requirements, and education courses. A class in instructional methods and one on human learning are included in this first term. One quick scan of Jean's calendar will tell anyone that she'll have little time to spare as she dives into her three-quarter program. Her friends entering the elementary education program will be immersed in a four-quarter program.

Whether students are in a quarter system, like Jean, or a semester arrangement, they generally will spend no more than a year and a half (more likely a year) to complete a secondary certification program, and no more than two years to complete an elementary program. Jean finds that about half of her classmates in the certification program already have finished their undergraduate degrees. So although her program is not a "fifth year" of course work and clinical experience like some advocate, it is approaching that.

Over 1200 institutions of higher education prepare teachers in the United States. Each program of preparation has a personality of its own, but each is reviewed and controlled, not by the profession itself, but by elected or appointed state boards of education, state superintendents, and regional accrediting agencies. Further, state legislatures have been quick to use their powers to mandate program elements as well as testing requirements in response to public concern about educational excellence in the 80's. Some of these requirements are oddities — the products of the idiosyncrasies of the legislative groups. But most of them are predictable: more specific coursework in methods, classroom management, needs of special students, reading; more field experience.

The key word is more, not different. Many educators have presented proposals for teacher education reform. It seems unlikely, however, that any of their truly innovative programs will become the rule in the future, unless state supervisory agencies can be convinced of the need for different qualities in the programs, not just more requirements, or unless teachers themselves can wrest control of certification and bring about a change.

Jean recognizes little of the difficulty surrounding reform of teacher education. As a student, she has not yet been introduced to the crucial political issues that surround her chosen profession. Even when the question arises in later coursework, the significance is likely to be lost on her. Few student teachers, indeed few practicing teachers, focus on such global issues no matter how important. Tomorrow's lessons take precedence.

And so in the first week of the term, Jean dutifully attends the classes required of her in a generally typical program of preparation. If we view Jean's program as Mary Kluender did in her study for the National Institute of Education, we must look at the total four- or five-year college program as the teacher education program. Kluender thus found that approximately forty percent of most prospective teachers' programs are really composed of general liberal arts studies; the first two years of college work would about equal this. Then, an additional component consists of work in a major and perhaps a minor field of specialization. Secondary teachers will do about 40 percent of their study here, while elementary teachers in many colleges put in about half that. Finally, elementary teachers spend about 45 percent of their program in actual professional education studies, while secondary teachers spend about 20 percent.

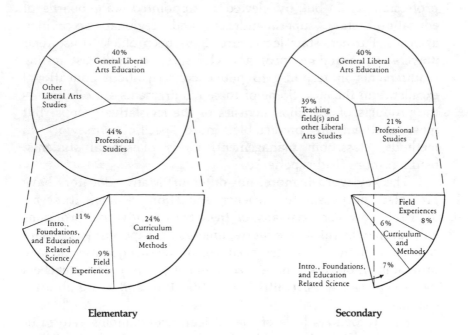

Elementary   Secondary

(Source: M. M. Kluender, *Journal of Teacher Education*)

Within the program of professional education studies, elementary education students take about half of their credits in curriculum and instructional methods courses, another one-fourth in foundational courses such as psychology, history, and philosophy, and the remainder in field experiences. Secondary students divide their much smaller number of credits almost equally among curriculum and methods, foundations, and field experiences.

Neither secondary nor elementary teachers actually spend much of their total college program studying professional knowledge. As many educators have pointed out, this too-brief introduction to teaching makes for incomplete skill development, shallow understanding of human learning, and partially completed socialization to the role. It also leads to a lack of reflection about one's teaching.

Brief preparation programs place tremendous responsibility for completing basic teacher education on the beginning teachers and on the organizations in which they are first employed. This on-the-job learning, often at the expense of large numbers of students, has been decried by countless educators, innumerable students and parents, and generations of beginning teachers. Beginning teacher assistance programs (discussed in the next chapter) have developed in part because of the brevity of preparation programs.

In the Field

After her first week of visits to the school, Jean would like to spend every spare moment there, but she has no car. She must depend on the city bus system to get her to and from the school. She is envious of several of her fellow students who have their own cars and thus more freedom to make their own flexible schedules. Staying after class to talk with her cooperating teacher takes real planning, so Jean feels deprived of the special opportunities to learn from spontaneous conversations that might happen if she didn't have to rush off to catch a bus back to campus.

The fact that Jean has begun her field experience at the same time that she has begun coursework makes her program among the less traditional, though by no means radically different. Traditional teacher preparation programs have been based on the theory-example-practice format. A program based on this format begins with coursework (the theory) including history, philosophy, and human learning, followed by observations (examples), capped with teaching in the field under supervision (practice). The theory-example-practice program is what John Dewey would have called an *apprenticeship* model. But Dewey also introduced another model that he called an *experiential*, or laboratory model.

This experiential model proposes a cycle which begins with an experience. The experience is followed by reflection, including interpretation, analysis and generalization. Reflection then is followed by application of the newly derived generalization while undergoing new but similar experiences. The cycle then repeats itself. A teacher education program based on this model would provide the student with an experience of teaching (early field experience, simulations or case studies) followed by individual reflection and group dialogue (interpretation, analysis, generalization), and then by another real or simulated experience (application), then more reflection. . . . Specific facts, concepts, and skills are learned from direct instruction, but they are considered supplementary to the reflective core. They are more often taught when the student has been led to recognize the need for them, often after guided reflection on teaching experiences.

It is this second model, an experiential program, that Jean is beginning. It demands not just more field experience, but also experiences that are distributed throughout the entire teacher education program. Traditional programs also have added more distributed field time in recent years. Such changes provide more skill building opportunities than before and give students early realistic experience in teaching to help them decide about continuing in the program. Some other programs have joined the "more field experience" bandwagon because it is the thing to do and not because of any particularly well-thought-out model for learning about teaching.

While distributed field experiences are one signal of an experiential program, other factors also must be examined to differentiate it from the traditional. For example, the experiential program has a clear linkage between field experience and seminars or other small group discussions. Courses offered progress from the more concrete instructional methods to the more abstract foundational courses, or intertwine the concrete and the abstract in blocks taught by teams composed of both instructional specialists and foundations experts. The overall program centers not so much on training for discrete competencies but on development of a repertoire of teaching behaviors that are outgrowths of thoughtful consideration of real experiences.

The experiential program is by far the more difficult to provide, because guiding reflection toward the development of the teacher as problem solver is labor-intensive, time-consuming, and exhausting. Experiential programs can drift easily if commitment is not regularly renewed. Students may even fight the experiential approach, for it may often seem "too theoretical" (meaning not immediately practical for the next day in class) to the beginners who are looking for immediate survival skills.

Jean, for example, knows she needs to work on her instructional skills, and she certainly agrees that she needs to know more about classroom management and about science, but she is not at all sure that the time spent in education class discussions, seminar dialogues and written assignments will be worth it. She wants action; talking, analyzing, considering, reconsidering all seems unnecessary when she thinks she needs concrete skills. Likewise, she can't quite see the need for the specialized terminology of education; it is what you do, not what you call it that matters.

The Critical Role of the Cooperating Teacher

Jean's cooperating teacher, Bob, is an enthusiastic science and mathematics teacher in his seventh year of teaching. Jean is Bob's first teacher education student, so he is not quite sure of his role. But he does believe that he should take as much time as possible to talk with her about the work of teaching. He remembers how painfully little attention he got from his own cooperating teacher and how awash he was on his own. He has been given no free time to work with Jean, so extended conversations must be stolen moments or combined with lunch. He wants Jean to observe him working with students, but he also believes she should get in "up to her elbows" as quickly as possible, so by the end of the first week she is assisting him with student projects on water pollution.

Jean is lucky to have an enthusiastic cooperating teacher. She expects her experience with him to prove satisfying. But there are some points of concern that should be noted. Bob has had virtually no orientation to the program in which he is now a critical participant, nor has he had training in supervision skills.

His views on teaching may be at odds with the views of Jean's instructors, his expectation of Jean unrealistic.

The unfortunate truth is that Bob is a typical cooperating teacher — willing but unprepared. His incentives for performing the role must be entirely personal. His state has set no standards and invested next to nothing in his selection or training as a cooperating teacher. (Only two states, West Virginia and Kentucky, have certification systems for cooperating teachers, while nine additional states require a course in supervision.) Further, his pay for working with Jean is miserably low — only $100 for three full quarters. He is not necessarily viewed as a master teacher because he has been assigned a student teacher. In fact, principals have been known to assign student teachers to incompetent teachers in hopes that the student may offset the problems created by the failures of the teacher. In other schools, the opportunity or responsibility of student teachers is passed around — a burden or a gift, depending on the outlook of the teachers.

That Bob is a good teacher and is happy to work with Jean is her good fortune and ours, for some research on teacher education programs points to cooperating teachers as among the most influential individuals in affecting student teachers' learning of the role and skills.

There is considerable disagreement about just how much effect teacher education programs or other teachers really have on any individual's learning of the teacher role. In 1932, Willard Waller argued that teachers are socialized by other teachers. But there are other perspectives. Some, like Dan Lortie, have argued that regardless of the people in them, teacher education programs have little or no effect. Instead, each individual's approach to the role of teacher has solidified long before entering a preparation program. Though the person may temporarily mimic the attitudes and behavior approved by a given program, he or she will return to original form when the program is finished and the need to pretend is gone. If that original form looks much like the other teachers with whom the new teacher works, it can be attributed to the fact that both teachers were influenced by similar models early in life, not to their effects on each other.

Others continue to believe that teacher preparation programs *can* transform individuals and instill understandings and beliefs which may not have been present before entering teacher education. Many modestly claim that teacher education programs can and do have a socializing influence, but that the degree of influence is due not only to the program, but also to the characteristics of the individuals, and to the contexts in which they try out the newly-found perspectives. Given a powerful, coherent *innovative* program that selects entrants differently, prepares them differently, and then provides a supportive context in which to solidify their new perspectives, a considerable effect might be felt.

Teacher educators may well be as conservative as practitioners in the field. Thus, while they claim to offer new ideas, they actually seek to instill traditional ones, after selecting students who are already most likely to embody traditional attitudes.

Studies of teacher socialization support an interactionist position that puts the individual, the teacher education curriculum, and the contextual influences as equal forces in role development. These studies demonstrate that experienced teachers and prospective teachers are not all influenced by the same people; their socializing agents can differ according to their own personal characteristics. They also can change over time. For example, Carolyn Bogad found that early deciders often are heavily influenced by their cooperating teachers, if the cooperating teachers are good. Others, like the crusaders and the converts are more likely to be influenced by their professional education faculty. But if the people in those socializing roles are weak, or if the prospective teacher carries a particularly strong image of the teacher he would like to be, he will develop a highly-personalized role.

As beginning teachers gain experience they respond differently to potential socializing agents like other teachers, administrators, parents, and students. Teachers' talk reveals that they pay more attention to praise and criticism from different groups in the later years than they had as beginners. But teachers are not all alike in focus in either the beginning or the later years. Their personal characteristics and the teaching situations in which they find themselves are powerful influences as well.

So, during her student teaching experience Jean may well be influenced by Bob, her cooperating teacher. But as a crusader she is likely to feel the strongest effect from her university instructors — if they are good. We might predict that if conflicts arise between what Bob espouses and what Jean hears in her classes she is likely to "side" with her instructors, though she may not behave that way in Bob's classroom.

It seems evident that if the teacher education curriculum, Jean's past store of knowledge and attitudes, and her field experiences all are greatly in conflict she will develop an idiosyncratic perspective on her work. She may decide that, given the lack of consensus, she is absolutely free not only to choose her own educational priorities without the need for defense, but also to choose whichever knowledge and skills of the craft she wishes to select — believing their use to be a matter of taste. Finally, she is likely to join a significant group of teachers who believe that no one can actually evaluate "good teaching," especially their own, and that there is little anyone can or should do to establish standards for entering the profession and remaining in it.

But for now, Jean is just beginning. She finds her instructors quite good. They are pleasant and task-oriented, and seem to have a clear image of the kinds of teachers they are aiming to prepare. They describe thinking teachers who aren't tied to a single approach, text or program. Though they do not always practice what they preach, they make a genuine effort. Of course there is the one whose own ineptness in the classroom makes a mockery of all the principles he and the others are teaching. Jean muses about how hard it must be to be a teacher of teachers, knowing that your every mistake in procedure could damage your credibility with your students.

Mid-term Stress

As the term proceeds, Jean is overwhelmed by her work load. The stress is incredible. She is not sure she can handle work like this. Assignments are due — lesson plans, micro-teaching sessions, observation reports. Tests are scheduled, and there is always the pull of the school and "her" students. She helps Bob lead a group of them on a weekend campout, an exhilirating time, but her own schoolwork has to be finished on Sunday night when she returns from the trek. Jean's seminar leader has warned them of this point in the term when, much like beginning teachers, they experience work overload and a flood of apprehension about themselves, their competence, and their role fit. She laughingly calls this state of mind "mental hyperventilation" and helps them talk through their fears.

Jean is beginning to realize that what had seemed natural and easy about instruction really requires a tremendous amount of preparation and practice. She sees Bob, with seven years of teaching experience, still spending time finding materials just right for his students, making up his own if none can be found, preparing lab equipment and supplies, writing quizzes and tests, then carefully correcting papers for hours, trying out different instructional approaches with each new class if the earlier ones didn't respond as he had hoped. By his example Bob is showing Jean what Christopher Clark had explained — that preparation for instruction is different from studying for a test, and that she has to think about the instructional process as much, if not more, than she thinks about subject matter. Clark and his colleagues would say that Jean's recognition of this fact places her well ahead of many less successful practicing teachers.

When her field supervisor schedules an observation when Jean is to teach a full lesson to the seventh graders, she is full of anxiety. But she manages to carry off the hour successfully, judging by the supervisor's comments during the conference afterward. She worried most about appearing professional, as Frances Fuller's work has predicted for someone at this stage of career development. The students, who seem to like Jean, were amazingly cooperative, almost as if they had conspired to make Jean look good. Of course, she and they are not conscious of the subtle ways they are already influencing her to become the kind of teacher with whom they can be comfortable, just as Elizabeth Eddy and Howard Becker found in their separate studies of beginning and experienced teachers in inner-city schools.

Coming to Enjoy Reflection

As the first term draws to a close, Jean has begun to look forward to the weekly seminars and the debates about curriculum and methods. She has a growing sense of her own power to analyze classroom situations and learning goals, generate alternative strategies for responding to them, and select approaches to try out. Somehow, having labels for the elements of teaching and learning has become more reasonable. It helps her to structure her thinking and be more precise in her work. She has begun to feel that she understands some things about how learning occurs and what actions she can take to guide that learning. Jean's needs for respect, liking, and competence are all being met by her experiences. Only her need for belonging is unsatisfied, for she still feels like an outsider among the teachers at the school — sometimes like an over-sized seventh grader. Maybe acceptance will come as she takes over more of Bob's teaching responsibilities.

Jean Continues the Program

Jean will be spending half her time in the field now that the second term has begun. She is enrolled in a curriculum and methods course in science, and is happy to finally begin to get a background in materials and methods special to her field. She also must take a course designed to teach her about testing and measurement (a class she's not so sure she really agrees is necessary). Finally, she must also make time for a required course that appears to combine history, philosophy and something called policy analysis. The content of this last "academic pedagogical knowledge" course, as B. O. Smith labels them, is the kind that is most likely to disappear in the alternative credentialing programs initiated in New Jersey, Virginia, and California in response to teacher shortages. Smith argues that such knowledge functions as the wellspring of hunches, the substance out of which policies are formed, and the ingredients which shape our decisions about teaching. But he also admits that few teachers and other school personnel understand the usefulness of this knowledge, and many in academic pedagogy don't either. Its loss in teacher education could well force the occupation into a narrow technical focus and thwart efforts toward professionalization.

Now Jean spends every morning at her school. Bob has agreed that she will be fully responsible for two important units. She also will be leading group discussions, giving demonstrations and working with students during the laboratory sessions, but these will still be under Bob's direction. Jean is concerned about her ability to lead discussions skillfully, so Bob wants to give her plenty of opportunity to work with small groups. He will not be free to observe her and give feedback in that situation, but he still thinks the experience will be educational. Even if Bob were free to observe Jean, he would be unlikely to approach the task with much enthusiasm. When he has observed her in the past he made some comments, but he didn't really offer the kind of critical evaluations that would help her improve her performance. But at least he had observed her a little. Jean knows of a fellow student who received a glowing written report from his cooperating teacher without ever having been observed by him!

In January, Bob's already limited planning time with Jean suddenly is cut in half as he is assigned to chair a district curriculum review committee. Certainly the curriculum work is important to the district, but the fact that administrators have requested Bob's help with it while he is working with a student teacher tells much about the value they place on well-supervised student teaching. Jean resents the encroachment on her time with Bob, but also realizes what a good opportunity the committee work is for him because he has expressed interest in becoming a principal. In some ways, Jean welcomes his new assignment, for it will mean he'll let her do more in the classroom without the fear of observable mistakes. So all are satisfied, but not all are best served.

The first of Jean's units begins. She tries a pretest of knowledge and skills necessary — a disaster. Half the students are ready, a fourth are hopelessly lacking in prerequisites, and a fourth already know much of what she thought she'd teach. How will she ever keep them all learning? A conference with her university science education professor helps. Still, as the unit gets underway, Jean can't believe how quickly things can disintegrate or how miraculously some lessons can right themselves. She is amazed at the effect her students can have on her sense of self. One day she finds herself elated with her success; the next she drags home feeling absolute defeat. Her fellow teacher education seminar members understand; sometimes their problems sound worse. She has nightmares about leading student discussions. In them, Bob, her field supervisor, and the principal are all watching. No one will talk; the students all shrug their shoulders and look vacant. She babbles on and on, afraid of silence.

The term scuttles by. Jean can't always see her own progress, but Bob and the field supervisor do during their few, short observations. They see, too, that her natural interest in her students is a real asset. Sometimes the time spent getting to know students seems more important to Jean than time spent learning the things her university professors think she needs. Some of it seems so utterly impossible to implement, even though it may sound great. Who has time to write tests so carefully? Who has time to individualize? She wonders cynically if physicians had to treat patients in groups of thirty, yet diagnose and prescribe

individually, just how successful they'd be. When she does try out
the recommended methods, they don't always work. Is she the
problem or is it the method? She'd rather not blame herself.

Student Teaching

Her final term! How far she has come in such a short time.
Jean doesn't recognize all the refinements in her approach to
teaching, but others do. As she prepares for her final full-time
student teaching, she has growing respect for the work teachers
do. Sometimes she gets discouraged, thinking she has made little
progress. She realizes how long it will take her to become the kind
of teacher she would like to be. Perhaps it is too idealized.
Sometimes it's all you can do to get a ditto master run!
Bob has turned everything over to Jean now. She is teaching
all his science classes and helping the P.E. teacher organize
intramural track and field activities after school. One of the
teachers who lives near the university gives Jean a ride home, so
she is free to stay and help. Bob sometimes observes her teach and
gives her praise, but he generally leaves her on her own while he
works in his small office in the rear of the classroom. He still helps
her in planning lessons and finding materials.
For help in instructional skills, Jean has come to count on her
field supervisor, who seems to be attuned to the kinds of questions
and problems Jean is having. Jean's supervisor was herself a high
school teacher, so she is knowledgeable about teaching and about
adolescents. Like an increasing number of supervisors, she has
been trained in clinical supervision skills including observation,
conferencing, and evaluation. She is not, like supervisors at most
universities, a subject-area specialist, but a generalist working with
student teachers who are all placed within certain assigned
schools. Neither the generalists nor the traditional subject-area
specialists, however valuable to student teachers, are given much
credit by the traditional university reward systems for their contributions. Unless teacher education programs are able to bring
greater rewards to field supervisors, it is unlikely that the best and
brightest teacher educators will choose supervision work.
Student-teaching full time now, Jean finds opportunities to
get to know a few other teachers at her school. She is delighted at
the humor with which they approach their work, at their sense of
purpose and commitment to teaching. They don't talk much about

their teaching, though, despite Jean's wishes that they would. She needs to hear how they solve problems with their students; she needs to know that she is not alone in her feelings and thoughts about her work. Jean does pick up on their involvement in their local professional teachers' organization and she begins to think more seriously about the role she'd like to play in such a group in the future. She observes, too, the quiet despair of some who seem to have resigned themselves to a colorless, plodding kind of teaching. Why do they stay? Why don't they do everyone a favor and leave?

As friendships grow with other teachers, contacts with the university are reduced. Although she makes a point to see her methods professor when she can, Jean's only regular ties to the university now are through her field supervisor and seminar leader, who continues to prod Jean and the others to think seriously about what is happening to them as they learn to be teachers. How are they changing? How are they growing?

Jean has seen several fellow students drop from the program. Some had gone because they discovered that the reality of teaching was far different from the picture they had imagined; some because they could not keep up the pace; some were asked to leave. Jean is most disturbed about the loss of a couple of bright mavericks whose personal styles and pointed questions made the professors embarrassed or defensive. Their questions about the inequities of the current school system disturbed Jean deeply. Who will raise those questions in the field now that they are gone?

Still, Jean really likes her fellow interns who remain. They have a growing kinship. They have admitted their defeats and offered helpful alternatives. They've celebrated small and large classroom triumphs, and debated educational issues with an increasing realization of their importance. They have come to be both more alike and more unique as they have struggled to find their own styles within the model of the reflective teacher espoused by the educators with whom they have worked.

In years past, Jean and her friends would have been seen as "inexperienced experts" armed with a full array of skills and knowledge, needing only that which experience mysteriously added to become full-fledged masters. Today, they are more readily acknowledged to be what Clark has called "well-started novices." They have had a general orientation to the profession; they possess some unpracticed pedagogical skills and some academic knowledge. More importantly, Clark, as Dewey before him, claimed that these novices should be seen as learners whose primary work was to continue their development toward expert status.

Jean and her friends are among the smaller number of students graduating from teacher education programs. New testing eliminates some, and new requirements may stop others. Teacher surplusses discouraged many from entering education programs in the late 70's and early 80's, and the growing attractions of other occupations have drawn away many women, minorities, and those in mathematics and science fields. Still, in the early 1980's, over 140,000 new teacher education graduates were added to the ranks each year. As the surplusses now turn to shortages and social forces again respond, the numbers may once again increase. Some predict that they will not rise fast enough to meet the growing need, however, and that alternative credentialing programs will increase. Innovative teacher education programs, temporary credentialing, and abbreviated programs, all designed to attract those already employed in other fields and those who might make other choices also are likely to increase.

But other old patterns change more slowly. In the near future, as today, three out of four of the new graduates will probably be women, and the majority of those women will prepare to be elementary teachers. Jean, aiming for a middle school position, will probably find herself in a school with about equal numbers of men and women. Her high school bound friends still will find male dominated faculties.

Selected References

Becker, H.S.   The Career of the Chicago Public School Teacher. *American Journal of Sociology.* 57, 1952. 470-477.

Beyer, L. E.   Field Experience, Ideology, and the Development of Critical Reflectivity. *Journal of Teacher Education* 35 (3) May/-June, 1984. 36-41.

Bogad, C. Recruitment and Socialization as Recurring Issues in Teacher Education. A paper presented at the annual meeting of the American Educational Research Association. New Orleans, Louisiana. 1984

Bowman, N.   College Supervision of Student Teaching: A Time to Reconsider. *Journal of Teacher Education.* 30 (3) May/June, 1979. 29-30.

Clark, C. Research on Teaching and the Content of Teacher Education Programs: An Optimistic View. A paper presented at the annual meeting of the American Educational Research Association. New Orleans, Louisiana, April 24, 1984.

Dewey, J. The Relation of Theory to Practice in Education. In *The Relation of Theory to Practice in the Education of Teachers.* The Third Yearbook of the National Society for the Scientific Study of Education, Part I. Bloomington, Illinois. 1904.

Eddy, E. *Becoming a Teacher.* New York: Teachers College Press, 1969.

Fink, C. H. Social Studies Student Teachers — What Do They Really Learn? A paper presented at the annual meeting of the National Council for the Social Studies. Washington, D.C. November, 1976. (ERIC document EJ 168 755).

Gehrke, N. J. A Grounded Theory Study of Beginning Teachers' Role Personalization Through Reference Group Relations *Journal of Teacher Education.* 32(6) November/December, 1981. 34-38.

Getzels, J. and H. Thelen. The Classroom as a Unique Social System. In *The Dynamics of Instructional Groups.* The Fifty-ninth Yearbook of the National Society for the Study of Education, Part II. Chicago, Illinois: University of Chicago Press, 1960.

Kluender, M. M. Teacher Education Programs in the 1980's: Selected Characteristics. *Journal of Teacher Education.* 35(4) July-August, 1984. 33-35.

Lortie, D., *Schoolteacher: A Sociological Study.* Chicago, Illinois: University of Chicago Press, 1975.

McIntyre, D. J. *Field Experiences in Teacher Education: From Student to Teacher.* Foundation for Excellence in Teacher Education & the ERIC Clearinghouse on Teacher Education. Washington, D.C. 1983.

Peterson P., R. W. Marx & C. M. Clark. Teacher planning, teacher behavior, and student achievement. *American Educational Research Journal.* 15, 1978. 417-432.

Sears, J. T.   Rethinking Teacher Education: Dare We Work Toward a
    New Social Order? *The Journal of Curriculum Theorizing.* 6 (2)
    Summer, 1985. 24-79.
Smith, B. O.   *A Design for a School of Pedagogy.* Washington, D.C.:
    U.S. Department of Education, 1980.
Waller, W. *The Sociology of Teaching.* New York, N.Y.: Russell and
    Russell, 1961.
Webb, C., N. Gehrke, P. Ishler, & A. Mendoza. *Exploratory Field Ex-
    periences in Teacher Education.* Association of Teacher Educators.
    Reston, Virginia. 1981. (ERIC document ED 205 482).
Zeichner, K. & R. Tabachnick.   Are the Effects of University Teacher
    Education "Washed Out" by School Experience? *Journal of Teacher
    Education..* 32(3) May/June, 1981. 7-13.
Zimpher, N. L., G. G. deVoss, & D. L. Nott.   A Closer Look at Univer-
    sity Student Teacher Supervision. *Journal of Teacher Education.* 31
    (4) July/August, 1980. 11-15.

3 BEGINNING

Hence young teachers are best; they are the most energetic, most intuitive, and the least resented.

Jacques Barzun
Teacher in America

Beginning to teach has been like closing one book and opening another. Beginning teachers had no further contact with their college or university faculty or super visors. At the same time, school districts did little with their new teachers. Beginning teachers entered their new positions energetic, intuitive, *and* on their own; their experiences too often were unpleasant.

An advertisement appearing in the Virginia Gazette, August 20, 1772, read:

Wanted Immediately
A Sober diligent Schoolmaster capable of teaching
Reading, Writing, Arithmetick, and the Latin Tongue.
The School is quite new, has a convenient Lodging
Room over it, is situated in a cheap Neighbourhood,
and its Income estimated at between sixty and eighty
Pound a Year. Any Person qualified as above, and well
recommended, will be put into immediate Possession of
the School, on applying to the Minister of Charles
Parish, York County. (cited by Willard Elsbree, 1939)

The speed with which the York County residents were willing to turn over possession of the school says much about the informal, undemanding process of evaluation for teacher applicants in that time. Two hundred years later, F. Howard Nelson's analysis of the data from the National Longitudinal Survey of the high school class of 1972 showed that within that carefully selected national sample "the lowest-scoring education graduates seem to be able to obtain teaching jobs as easily as other education graduates and garner the same salary" (p. 140). That this occurred during a time when these young people "faced the worst market for teachers since the Depression" should force us to scrutinize our teacher education programs as well as our teacher hiring practices. There are, in fact, signs of increasing attention to the quality of beginning teachers.

Today, when many teacher candidates locate possible positions, they face several additional challenges before the positions are theirs. Though some school districts still have simple procedures with limited interviews (the good opinion of one person may be sufficient), an increasing number have rigorous, complex reviews. Screening committees composed of specially trained teachers, administrators and community members interview prospective teachers at length, review writing samples and transcripts, observe the candidates' teaching, and then arrive at their decision. Teachers who have passed through this thorough review are likely to think of themselves in a considerably different light from those who gained their jobs through less demanding processes. When you successfully compete against many other applicants, you "take possession of the school" with increased self-confidence and enthusiasm.

Of course, all good intentions to improve teacher hiring practices so that the best are most likely to be hired can be undermined by teacher shortages. In times of shortage in the past, schools have had no choice but to hire whomever they might find, without the opportunity to be selective. We once again see such shortages in several areas of the country and are told that the problem will increase dramatically within the decade. Without extensive, immediate intervention, one might safely predict that those who are then pressed into taking possession of the schools will include a larger percentage of the less capable than Nelson found in the mid-1970's.

Beginning

"Taking possession of the school" may sound old-fashioned, but for the beginning teacher the words still ring true. Receiving the keys to the school is a significant experience:

I enjoyed it so much. I got my keys that day . . . I was so proud. This is my room! This is my drama room!

Always before, being in a school had meant being a student. Even student teachers are still students first. Rarely do they have open access to the school or claim possession of a classroom in the same way that teachers may. For a young beginning teacher, being entrusted with the keys to the school is a rite of passage signifying transition to adult status; for a more mature beginner, the keys may represent delayed attainment of a dream. In either case the passing of the keys marks the beginning of a new role in which the teacher must take charge, must appear knowledgeable, professional, caring, patient, creative, and fair. Above all *she must not act like a beginner!*

Trial By Fire

Other professions and skilled occupations allow for phases of varying length which recognize the novice status of the beginner. The journeyman, the intern, the resident, the junior partner, all designate one who is still in the early stages of learning, still under the more careful supervision of a senior practitioner. But the beginning teacher is on her own. Armed with the skills and concepts acquired in a brief training period, and fortified with the determination to make learning happen, beginning teachers courageously unlock the doors to their classrooms and try to do it all. Orientations for beginning teachers often consist of one or two days of general information about the school and district before the other teachers arrive. Supervision and follow-up have been nearly nonexistent. Not surprisingly, accounts of beginners' traumas have been the subject of several studies.

In 1966 Dan Lortie wrote of the isolated socialization of the beginning teacher — what he called the "Robinson Crusoe" model. He described the loneliness of the beginners even amidst the many children who surround them daily. Elizabeth Eddy, writing in

1969, told of the experiences of twenty-two first year teachers assigned to junior high and elementary positions in high-minority, low income areas of a large urban school district. She described the process of making a transition from the status of student to that of teacher, saying:

> *This is not an easy transition in any case, but it is especially difficult in the school in the slum area because the newcomer often encounters unfamiliar behavior on the part of pupils and sometimes on the part of others in the school. Yet here, as in other schools, new teachers find those who try to reach out and help them through what all agree is a difficult year. (p. 6-7)*

Lortie's and Eddy's studies pointed up the critical roles played by students, principals, and other teachers in socializing the beginning teacher to life in a particular school.

In 1970, Kevin Ryan offered the descriptions of first year experiences of six beginning teacher interns along with his own comments in *Don't Smile Until Christmas*. His beginners' journals exemplified the rollercoaster experiences of the first year. In later studies in the 1970s Ryan and others have drawn attention to the powerful effects the school environment and personal lives of beginning teachers can have on their success in the classroom. More recently Carl Glickman (1985) described the phenomenon of *inverse beginner responsibilities* in which:

> *. . . administrators often place the most difficult and lowest achieving students with the new teacher . . . The message to beginning teachers is, 'Welcome to teaching. Let's see if you can make it.' . . . If new teachers do make it, they pass their initiation rites onto the next group of beginners. (pp. 38-39)*

Simon Veenman of The Netherlands has synthesized the research on problems of beginning teachers, including work from Western Europe, Australia, and North America (1984). His review finds that beginners everywhere experience reality shock due to problems ranging from discipline to instructional materials; there is, it seems, almost no area in which beginners *do not* have problems.

As they take possession of the schools, however, most new teachers are unaware of the traumas that lie ahead. During the first week or two of teaching they experience a honeymoon period. In the whirlwind of activity produced by the start of the school year the euphoric beginner can hardly imagine that others have found the first year to be so grim. Stressful, yes, but not grim. How could anyone be isolated and lonely? Fellow teachers seem ready to loan materials, to share ideas. The principal often is solicitous and supportive. The secretary shows you the ropes. The students show a normal range of exuberance. If you are young, you may find it easy to relate to the students as a big brother or sister; if more mature, by assuming the parent role. Family members and friends are curious about your experiences and seem to delight in the stories you relate. You're doing what you want to do, and all is right with the world!

Now of course there are exceptions to this idyllic scene. Some beginners walk into situations that would be difficult for even the most experienced of teachers. They find surprise assignments, over-crowded classes, hostile students, apathetic colleagues, a burned out principal, a surly custodian, insufficient textbooks, no permanent classroom, a crumbling building. Beginners facing these challenges "get realistic" much more quickly than their honeymooning counterparts, but they are hardly better off for it.

Disenchantment

The unfortunate fact is that beginning teachers under both conditions often seem to reach a period of disillusionment by about the sixth week of school. The work of social-psychologist Saul Levine assures us that this phase is common in human adaptation to new lives. He describes this characteristic disorganization as the first of four phases, followed by a short "acting out" phase in which the person copes by becoming uninvolved and/or somewhat exploitative of others. A longer period of "searching" then follows during which the individual reexamines his life in a less frenetic manner. Finally the phase of "adaptation and integration" may be reached. Here the person can find total involvement in the new life.

The time of disenchantment arrives whether the beginning teacher is younger or older, male or female, elementary or secondary, perceptive or unaware. This period may be more or less severe, longer or shorter, but it happens to nearly every new teacher. There is no single cause. It is the result of several forces combining to reach a critical level about the sixth week.

One of the first things the beginning teacher notices is that people within the school withdraw their support. Colleagues and administrators may have been helpful and caring initially, but they stop actively offering help after the first two to three weeks. They do not stop out of malice. They probably are not even conscious of the change. As they bring order to their own school work, they assume the beginner also has gained control and no longer needs their help — in fact, might resent their offer. Teachers value independence. If they want it for themselves, they believe others do also. To offer help is to intervene and thus reduce independence. They are busy people too, so they stop offering. But the beginner would like help:

> I wouldn't mind if someone came in and gave me pointers . . . I don't know if I'm ready for the principal, but I'm floundering . . . I talked to others and they feel the same.

At the same time, family and friends lessen their support. The funny stories about the students, the personality sketches, the mixups and confusions were amusing to them at first, but they find little entertainment in the teacher's rapidly developing problems. "How can you make such a big deal out of a relationship with a twelve-year old? How can you get so upset over something so trivial?"

Family and friends also begin to resent the powerful intrusion of school in their lives. It is not just the teacher's preoccupation with kids, colleagues and school events; it is also the teacher's need to deal with paperwork. The omnipresent stack of papers to be corrected and daily lessons to be planned are visible signs to living partners that they now must share time with a group of strangers. They may be noticeably jealous and resentful. One teacher reported that after only two weeks her husband, who had been unhappy about her plan to teach anyway, said, "When do you think you're going to get fed up with this?" Her daughter claimed to feel "neglected."

Older beginning teachers with spouses and children have the most trouble here, especially women. But young teachers do not escape unscathed. New spouses and roommates can be equally unsympathetic, demanding, and insensitive. If one lives alone the situation is different, but not necessarily better; there is no one to talk to in either case. The most fortunate beginning teachers are those who are married to or have strong friendships with teachers; the shared occupation gives license to talk about work.

As support from friends and colleagues withers, the teacher enters a time when she needs it even more. She is exhausted from long days at school followed by late nights at the kitchen table correcting papers.

> *I get home and I'm tired. Every night I walk in the door and the kids say, "You've got to take me somewhere." That's irritating. I'm tired, I get home, and I still do two or three hours of work at home.*

She is well aware that her performance is now being evaluated. Now her mistakes and problems can have serious consequences. Now any admission of need, any requests for help can be viewed as an exhibition of weakness.

> *I didn't get it. Now I feel like an idiot going in to get it straightened out.*

She cannot ask, or if she does, it can only be about those items about which a beginner would obviously not know — Where is this? Who handles that? What is the procedure here?

They do not ask, "How can I make them listen? How can I make them learn?" They are supposed to know that already. But *that* is exactly where there is trouble, for the students have begun to discover the soft spots. They have tested the teacher and have found vulnerabilities. They talk back; they act out; they come late; they don't do the work; they say they don't understand; they fool around; they fail tests. The pressure to develop daily lessons that are both motivating and worthwhile in the face of apparent student disinterest is overwhelming.

> *I'm dull. I just don't feel I'm very dynamic . . . I still don't sleep nights . . . I'm walking around in a daze half the time . . . I wake up quite often at night and I have my teeth clenched . . . I've had some headaches that just go on . . . I'm not what I'd like to be, but I don't know how to go about changing.*

Even if the students are interested, the sheer volume of work seems impossible.

> *I get here early; I don't really mind that. It doesn't bother me to stay until four. What bothers me is going home and having more work to do . . . until 10:00.*

And so in the span of a few short weeks many beginners go from the zenith of optimism to the depths of despair. Kevin Ryan and his colleagues found that not all the beginning teachers in their study reported low points at about six weeks. Some experienced earlier lows (even prior to the opening of school). Others reported lows in the second half of the year. Still, a sizeable group reported that their greatest problems came in October, November, and December, which is about when Lagana had earlier claimed the downward "curve of disenchantment" was noticeably steep. This manic-depressive pattern may be surprising to no one. What *is* surprising is that most beginning teachers survive it and continue to teach.

Picking Up the Pieces

The beginners keep on. In themselves and through others they find the strength to handle the challenges presented by their students, to deal with the delicate balancing of home and school life, to face the reality of the solitary, often capricious nature of teaching. Saul Levine claims that the period of disorganization varies in length and intensity, but is especially dependent:

> . . . *on the nature of the people that the individual meets and lives with. A firm sense of belonging in highly valued groups enables more effective coping . . . (Also) adequate preparation beforehand often obviates many of the disabilities of this stage. (p. 216)*

If the beginners are among the fortunate who work in schools where the needs of novice teachers are recognized, they may find that they are really not alone, that they are not expected to know it all, and that there are many who will help them begin to shape themselves into the teachers they wish to become. Such beginning teacher programs, popular in the 60's, have once again found favor. Mention of several exemplar programs will give an idea of the nature of these attempts.

One project of the Research and Development Center for Teacher Education at the University of Texas at Austin was focused on the development of a model teacher induction program through a network of satellite projects based across the nation. State-wide projects can be found in growing numbers. A support program in Washington state was piloted during the 85-86 school year. In this program, 200 beginning teachers have been matched with helping teachers (mentors) who provide individualized support without the threat of evaluation for employment. By its second year the project will serve 800 beginning teachers. In Wisconsin a similar state-wide project is underway; likewise in North Carolina, South Carolina, and Georgia. Oklahoma is entering its fourth program year.

Collaborative programs between colleges and school districts are also frequent. In one such program Phillip Schlechty worked with the Charlotte-Mecklenburg School District to create a career development program to provide special help in classroom instruction for novice teachers. The novices are called "provisional teachers" in a six-level career ladder, and are given special training, support, and individualized help by teachers ranked higher on the career ladder.

The Toledo Internship-Intervention Program is yet another promising program to work with beginning teachers and experienced teachers whose skills are weak. The difference in this program is that it was initiated and developed by the Toledo Federation of Teachers, an American Federation of Teachers affiliate, and not by administrators from the school district. It depends on the peer-supervision skills of carefully selected consulting teachers who work with each beginning teacher to identify goals, then carry out detailed observations and follow-up conferences to improve the teacher's planning and instruction. Begun in 1981, the Toledo program is a fine example of teachers taking charge of their own profession.

In general these programs to help beginning teachers often include not only formal, continuing instruction in the skills of teaching — skills that may have been introduced, but not perfected during preservice programs — but also informal support networks to reduce the isolation felt by many novices. Small seminar-like sessions in which the beginners can express their feelings, ask questions without hesitation, describe their problems, and offer help to others seem to ease the passage into the teacher role. So does having a more experienced teacher who isn't just available when asked, but who stays tuned to needs, offers help before asked, is quick to praise and a patient listener, and doesn't resort to pat answers to difficult questions. Principals and other supervisors who have been carefully prepared to offer supervision and to evaluate the beginner as a beginner are another component of thoughtfully developed programs for induction.

Many of the new induction programs not only show an awareness of the needs of teachers in adapting to new lives, but also attend to the research on phases of teacher development and adult learning. Beginning with the work of Frances Fuller, educators have examined the differences in teacher concerns at different stages in their careers. They have discovered that as teachers gain experience in the classroom, their concerns turn gradually away from self to student learning. Knowing this, and that adult learners prefer much more control over the focus and direction of learning, programs such as the one in Toledo have emerged that acknowledge the beginners' concerns and give each beginner a greater role in the selection of skills and knowledge to be strengthened and in the methods for doing so.

Newer programs also acknowledge that all beginners are not alike, that often older novices share characteristics with more experienced teachers, because they are in a similar life stage, different from the young beginner. For example, many older novices have children of their own. This fact is perceived by teachers themselves as significant in changing their approach to teaching according to both Lightfoot and Spencer. Margaret Cohen's study of college-aged and older-adult preservice teachers concluded that the two groups differed in their commitment to teaching and in their focus on interpersonal relationships with students. Older preservice teachers were higher on the former, while college-aged preservice teachers were higher in the latter.

Age is not the only dimension on which beginning teachers differ from one another, and on which differences in inservice programs may be based. Certainly, the kinds of students and location of the school, the nature of one's preservice preparation, and the type of teaching assignment all affect the teacher's needs. Further, the kinds of people who are influential as socializing agents, the approach to problems, the ideal toward which the teacher strives, and the motives to teach all will differ from teacher to teacher.

What we see, in short, is that the more we look, the less likely we are to see a beginning teacher who can be easily categorized, whose first year experiences can then be seen as typical, and for whom we can then offer a prepackaged initiation program guaranteed to be successful in the integration of the beginner into life as a teacher. Programs of initiation are in order, but they must be responsive in the same way that we ask teachers to offer responsive programs of instruction to children.

Hanging on Until Summer

Beginning teachers look forward to the end of school as much as their students. They may need the summer break even more! Of course there have been enjoyable moments, successes with difficult students, words of praise from a supervisor, warm appreciation from a grateful parent, giggled thank-yous of self-conscious students, growing friendships with colleagues. Most new teachers plan to return the following year, and most do. But the year has taken its toll. Studies show that during the year they have become less idealistic, often less student-centered, more concerned with discipline, more satisfied with smaller successes. At the end of the year one woman focused on discipline, saying:

> I think I was too lenient [in the beginning]. Everyone had told us 'clamp down hard at first, and then you can easily let up' . . . I wasn't as strict in classroom behavior as I have learned since. I allowed ten or so minutes when I'd finish up early, and let them have the time. Kids took advantage of that. I used to accept late work. Now I don't.

A male high school teacher spoke of discipline and shifting responsibility:

> At the beginning of the year I thought it was maybe just new teachers who had problems, but it's all teachers. I think at the beginning of the year I placed too much of the blame for the kid's behavior on myself, whereas now, I don't know if it's good or bad; from talking to other teachers I see that it's the kids, not just my lack of control.

Being able to share the blame for failures is an adjustment that may be both good and bad. It may be good in that the teacher, by being relieved of the impossible burden of perfection (Reaching all, Teaching all), can live a more normal, less guilt-ridden life and therefore be freer to teach. It may be bad in that some teachers begin to see themselves as babysitters, at best. They relieve themselves of any responsibility for student behavior or student learning. Once this happens the teacher loses the will to invest in real teaching. A weary beginning teacher observed:

> I'm not so concerned about the job anymore. If everything is going to be a babysitting job — you sit

here and control the kids — then maybe I'll go do
something else . . . or go somewhere else where you
have kids who are more responsive, because these kids
are just unresponsive!

The teachers learn to submerge their feelings and strive to
compartmentalize episodes so that they don't harm their relationship with one student or class because of a problem with
another. At year end one woman explained:

I hope that I don't get as uptight as I did in the begin-
ning. Sometimes I took it out on the classes. If I had a
really bad time the hour before, the next class better
watch it . . . In the beginning I took each hour and
overlapped them — locked them into each other.

This compartmentalization probably protects students, but the demand on the teacher to appear outwardly calm, while inwardly
churning is immense and, over the years, is responsible in part for
the high level of stress-related illnesses reported by teachers and
documented by many studies such as those by Mason, Kaplan,
and Coates and Thoresen.

So beginning teachers welcome the last day of school. It is
the closing of the very critical first chapter. But as they speak with
relief of bringing the year to a close, they also look with barely-
contained enthusiasm to next year, to the ideas they'd like to try,
to the changes they've learned are necessary, to starting fresh with
a new class.

Selected References

Coates, T. J. and C. E. Thoresen. Teacher Anxiety: A Review with Recommendations. *Review of Educational Research.* Spring, 1976. 46 159-184.

Cohen, M. W. Teacher Career Development: A Comparison of College-aged and Older-Adult Preservice Teachers. A paper presented at the Annual Meeting of the American Educational Research Association. New York, 1982.

Darling-Hammond, L. *Beyond the Commission Reports: The Coming Crisis in Education.* Santa Monica, California: The Rand Corporation. July, 1984.

Eddy, E. *Becoming A Teacher.* New York: Teachers College Press, 1969.

Elsbree, W. S. *The American Teacher.* New York: American Book Co., 1939.

Fuller, F. F. Concerns of Teachers: A Developmental Conceptualization. *American Educational Research Journal.* March, 1969. 6: 207-226.

Glickman, C. D. The Supervisor's Challenge: Changing the Teacher's Work Environment. *Educational Leadership.* December 1984/ January 1985. 42 (4) 38-40.

Huling-Austin, L., G. E. Hall and J. J. Smith. A Collaborative Satellite Effort: Developing and Implementing a Model Teacher Induction Project. A paper presented at the Annual Meeting of the Association of Teacher Educators. Las Vegas, Nevada, 1985.

Kaplan L. *Mental Health and Human Relations in Education.* New York: Harper & Bros., 1959.

Levine, S. V. Draft Dodgers: Coping with Stress, Adapting to Exile. In R. Moos (Ed.) *Human Adaptation: Coping with Life Crises.* Lexington, Mass.: Health, 1976. 213-222.

Lagana, J. *What Happens to the Attitudes of Beginning Teachers.* Danville, Illinois: Interstate Printers & Publishers, Inc., 1970.

Lightfoot, S. L. The Lives of Teachers. In L. Shulman & G. Sykes (Eds.) *Handbook of Teaching and Policy.* New York: Longman, 1983. 241-260.

Lortie, D. Teacher Socialization: The Robinson Crusoe Model. In H. J. Hermanowitz (Ed.) *The Pluralistic World of the Beginning Teacher.* Washington D.C.: National Education Association, 1966.

Mason, F. V. A Study of Seven-Hundred Maladjusted School Teachers. *Mental Hygiene.* 1931. 15: 576-599.

Nelson, F. H. New Perspectives on the Teacher Quality Debate: Empirical Evidence From the National Longitudinal Survey. *Journal of Educational Research.* February 1985. 78 (3) 133-140.

Ryan, K. *Don't Smile Until Christmas.* Chicago: University of Chicago Press, 1970.

Ryan, K. Some Feedback is Better Than Others: Implications of a Study of First Year Teachers for the Follow-Up of Teacher Education Graduates. In *Implications of Experience in Teacher Education Program Follow-Up Studies for Future Work.* Austin, Texas: The Research & Development Center for Teacher Education, 1979. 5-24.

Ryan, K. and others. *Biting the Apple: Accounts of First Year Teachers.* New York: Longman, Inc., 1980.

Schlechty, P. C., A. W. Joslin, S. E. Leak, R. C. Hanes. The Charlotte-Mecklenburg Teacher Career Development Program. *Educational Leadership.* December 1984/January 1985. 42 (4) 4-8.

Spencer, D. A. The Home and School Lives of Women Teachers. *Elementary School Journal.* 1984. 84 (3) 283-298.

Veenman, S. Perceived Problems of Beginning Teachers. *Review of Educational Research.* Summer, 1984. 54 (2) 143-178.

Waters, C. M. and T. L. Wyatt. Toledo's Internship: The Teacher's Role in Excellence. *Phi Delta Kappan.* January, 1985. 66 (5) 365-367.

4 CONTINUING

. . . it takes the stubborness of a saint coupled with the imagination of a demon for a teacher to pursue his art of improvisation gracefully, unwearyingly, endlessly.

Jacques Barzun
Teacher in America

A teacher's sense of humor returns during the second year. Or maybe teachers acquire a sense of humor that year. It comes of necessity, or it comes because there is opportunity. Whatever the explanation, a sense of humor—the ability to laugh at self and the craziness of the human condition—is an element that career teachers cannot do without, not in the early years of survival and adjustment and not in the later years of continued teaching. In this chapter we look at those continuing years of teaching and why that sense of humor is so important. Though it is not possible to portray an entire career in a few pages, we can look at the general nature of teaching and then focus on what keeps some teachers exciting to their students and enthusiastic about their work year after year.

The Rewards and Challenges of Teaching

Experienced teachers agree that their largest measure of satisfaction comes from interacting with students. They chose to become teachers in order to work with young people; they continue to teach for the same reason. Their involvement is not just for the fun of conversation. It has a purpose—helping each student learn to grow up. In the large study that resulted in *A Place Called School,* John Goodlad and his colleagues questioned over 1300 teachers. More than half of the teachers claimed their prime reason for choosing teaching and remaining in it was the intrinsic reward of the work itself. In like manner, elementary *and* secondary teachers I have talked with say again and again something like:

> *It's a great feeling to see a student at the beginning of the school year, then see how much he progresses throughout the year.* That *to me is satisfying.*

The satisfaction of knowing that you have played some part in the progress of even a single student is powerfully rewarding. Once past the anxieties of the first year, teachers can focus on such rewards. But first year teachers often are so serious about their work, so serious about themselves, and so worried about success, that there is little time for personal satisfaction. And there is little need for any senior colleague to offer the traditional "Don't smile until Christmas" advice. Beginners scowl; they rush; they bark commands; they refuse to laugh at students' antics; they often are rigid and merciless.

Instructional communication researchers have found that many of the angry-looking behaviors are really anxiety responses, but the students can't tell the difference.

A second year teacher may be more of a disciplinarian, but the role is carried off without what Kevin Ryan calls "the sense of impending crisis." Paul Burden, who has interviewed teachers at many stages in their careers, says that teachers thought that they expressed more of their own personalities in the classroom after the first year. They let themselves be more open and genuine with children. They seemed to be less concerned about themselves: they seemed to have more time to enjoy teaching.

Changing concerns. Teachers' concerns change over time. As early as the 1960's Frances Fuller discovered that teachers move through several stages in their teaching concerns. Initially they center their thoughts on the way they appear to others, often without relevance to teaching. Next they turn to concerns about their adequacy as teachers, worrying about discipline and subject matter adequacy. Finally they resolve most of their concerns about themselves and turn to concerns about their students' learning. This concerns continuum is replayed in miniature each time a teacher faces a new situation in teaching, according to Gene Hall and Susan Loucks, who have looked at teachers' concerns in relation to staff development planning.

Frantic pace and crowding. Teaching is an occupation with a frantic pace for both beginners and the experienced. Thomas Cypher and Donald Willower observed high school teachers for a week in order to determine what kinds of activities absorbed the teachers' time during the work day. The teachers averaged 159 verbal exchanges each day during instruction time and 68 additional, brief (less than 1 minute) exchanges per day outside the class. In addition, unscheduled meetings longer than a minute averaged nearly 25 per week. Only 3.5% of the teachers' time was given to private time, time not spent in school-related tasks. Teachers hurry everywhere. One experienced high school teacher described her previous year this way.

> *It was a typical year in teaching — just a roller coaster ride you're constantly on. And you just have to make up your mind that you're going to be on it or else you just, I don't know, become insensitive.*

The work of elementary teachers is somewhat different—a smaller number of students to work with, somewhat more control over pace and rhythm—but the quantity of interactions and the lack of private time are similar. Ann Lieberman and Lynne Miller likened teaching in an elementary classroom to working in a three-ring circus because individual students or groups often work on completely different activities all at the same time. The teacher must keep track of everything and everyone, she must be "with it" as Jacob Kounin said it.

Phillip Jackson concluded that there still were many similarities in "life in classrooms" for teachers and students and that "school is school, no matter where it happens." He concluded that teachers are both hurried and crowded:

> *There is a social intimacy in schools that is unmatched elsewhere in our society. Buses and movie theaters may be more crowded than classrooms, but people rarely stay in such densely populated settings for extended periods of time and while there, they usually are not expected to concentrate on work or to interact with each other. . . . . Only in schools do thirty or more people spend several hours each day literally side by side. (page 8)*

Boredom. Given the crowding and hectic pace in schools, it may seem that teachers rarely would be bored. But boredom occurs. The first year may be full of new experiences, but with each passing year the search for the surprising, for the different can be increasingly difficult. New students come each year, and they are unique in many ways. But they are increasingly predictable. Sometimes there are new textbooks and new materials, but the objectives and content are similar from year to year. Sometimes a teacher gets a new grade level or a new classroom, but nearly always the same school, often the same colleagues. A fifth year English teacher complained:

> *Just generally, I'm tired of it, but I have mixed feelings. Five years is a long time to teach one subject. . . .I think maybe it's just subject that has me more discouraged than anything else. I'm tired of teaching the same thing.*

Five years *is* a long time to teach the same thing. When teachers retire after an uninterrupted career of 35 years in the first grade or a world history classroom, it is almost incomprehensible. Yet many do stay that long; a significant number at least twenty years. According to figures from the NEA, the average age of teachers in 1981, was 39, up from earlier years when most teachers were under 30. In some stable and shrinking school districts the average teacher age has reached 55 in recent years. While some of those teachers entered teaching later in life, most began as young college graduates.

Guilt. Teachers fight not only boredom during their careers, many also deal with a considerable amount of guilt. The guilt begins in the first year as teachers begin to recognize that they are not doing everything they know they could to "reach each student" as some ideal teacher would. They can forgive themselves a bit that first year because they are beginners and don't have everything together yet. But as time goes on the guilt at not doing everything possible can begin to tear at a teacher's sense of competence. Arthur Jersild talks of guilt in his thoughtful book, *When Teachers Face Themselves*, based on interviews and surveys of hundreds of teachers. Jersild relates the guilt feelings to feelings of hostility and anger turned inward, against the self—a punishing of self. Dan Lortie found a "torrent of feelings and frustrations" when he asked teachers about evaluating their success in teaching. One of the several teachers he quoted declared:

> *I always feel that if I'm not succeeding with some child it's my fault, that I should be able to find some way to appeal to him and make him want to do. You get a little discouraged. You think, well I'm no good as a teacher and then you have some children who do get it, and you think, well it can't be all my fault. (Lortie, 1975, p. 144)*

To balance the guilt they feel at failure with a few, teachers must keep in mind the successes they have had with others. Some days successes are great: a child reads unaided for the first time; a whole class demonstrates mastery of a complex concept; a usually unruly student leads a group project. Some days the successes are small, but enough: everyone handed in papers on time; no one had to be sent to the principal.

Isolation. Finally, there is the isolation of teaching. Many references attest to the fact that in the midst of all those students, teachers often feel alone, isolated from other adults with whom they might share their daily concerns, thorny problems, and small victories. Many teachers are physically isolated because their rooms are located at the ends of hallways, in out-of-the-way wings, or in "portables." Others are isolated by schedule or by lack of time. One experienced teacher lamented:

> *It's just—I really don't have anybody here. . . . I really don't get close to people at school because I have no time. I really don't have time.*

Still other teachers feel a kind of loneliness due to a lack of common interests with colleagues at their school or self-imposed constraints resulting from fears of judgment. Jersild claimed that this loneliness arises "because there is a rift within oneself or because there is something strange and alien in one's relation to others." As one teacher speculated:

> *I think sometimes teachers hide what they feel; they hide their disappointments. They are afraid to show their lack of ability in some areas. They are afraid to be wrong.*

Isolation from other adults makes some teachers worry that they will come to think and talk like their students instead of the reverse.

The changing occupation. In addition to the common problems of teaching, many teachers face the added difficulties of being part of a changing occupational group. Although unionization of the work force of teachers has had benefits, it also has brought with it the unhappy experience of strikes, grievances and labor disputes. A more negative public attitude about teachers and their effectiveness has put teachers in a particularly defensive posture. Many report feeling a lack of respect for the accomplishments they can rightfully claim. More than a decade of declining enrollment has meant a decrease in new teachers, and hence the loss of the vital enthusiasm they bring. It also has meant school closures, staff reductions, and involuntary transfer to positions which teachers may neither have desired nor felt qualified to fill.

Toward Renewal and Growth

A sense of humor, then, is a necessary response to the hurrying, crowding, invaded privacy, fragmentation, monotony, guilt and isolation, and the negative outcomes of a changing profession. As one wise experienced teacher declared:

> *I still believe that one of the most important things that a teacher must keep is a sense of humor, especially about himself.*

Humor soothes daily difficulties, relieves tensions and gives teachers some perspective on their work. But renewing enthusiasm for work from day to day and year to year, countering the stress from years of crowding and lack of privacy, and responding to the need to fight fragmentation take more than a healthy sense of humor. These things require a belief that the rewards of teaching far outweigh the problems. More important, they require a growth-oriented perspective on teaching—teaching as becoming rather than being—moving rather than "stuck" (to use Rosabeth Kanter's terminology).

Over the past few years, as more teachers have stayed in teaching longer, researchers have begun to look in new ways at the work and lives of continuing teachers. They have looked, not just to find what the problems may be, but also at what seems to help teachers sustain the sense of growth and fulfillment in teaching that is so necessary to productive, enthusiastic work with young people.

Three themes in this research on teachers stand out. The first is the development of the teacher as a *reflective practitioner* or *researcher*, an outgrowth of the belief that good teachers must first be good learners. The second is the teacher as a *skilled practitioner* or *artisan*. This theme arises from the inquiry into the knowledge bases of teaching. The third theme is teacher as *whole person* whose life beyond school—family, community, world—affects the success and satisfaction of the teaching experience. These interlocking themes can serve as organizers for looking at what we know and what we still need to know about the continuing, growing teacher.

The Teacher as Reflective Practitioner

In recent years we have been reminded of Dewey's 1904 dictum that teacher education should aim to help teachers understand the underlying principles of practice, not just technical procedures. Scholars have termed teachers who strive for such understanding "teachers-as-researchers," "teacher-scholars," teachers-as-participant-observers," "self-monitoring teachers," and most recently "reflective teachers." As Jesse Goodman describes them, these reflective practitioners are individuals who regularly question what they are doing in the classroom, whether their actions are justified in relation to some rational theoretical model, and whether their actions are not only technically skilled, but also ethically sound.

The ability to be reflective is linked to cognitive development. And teachers vary a good deal in cognitive development, according to such researchers as David Hunt, Marilyn McKibbin & Bruce Joyce. Each of these researchers claims that teachers who operate at a higher level of cognitive function "perform in the classroom in a manner that fits closely with clusters of behaviors associated with effective teaching." (Sprinthall and Thies-Sprinthall, p. 19). In other words, it appears that teachers who are reflective, who function at a higher level, are better teachers.

Cognitive growth can be enhanced among adults. Lois Thies-Sprinthall summarized the conditions needed for such growth. They include the following:

- Placing persons in qualitatively significant role-taking experiences.
- Offering careful and continuous guided reflection.
- Balancing real experiences and discussion of them.
- Providing instruction that is both personally supportive and challenging.
- Offering continuous programs lasting at least six months to a year or more.

Educators have long sought to develop teacher education programs based on the concept of reflective teaching. The works of Dewey in 1904, Stratemeyer in 1956, Zeichner in 1981 and Cruickshank in 1985, all attest to that intent. But more recently educational theorists also have considered the continued development of reflective experienced teachers as well. Teachers are not thought to be finished growing when they get their certificates. Staff development programs have been created based on the assumption that some teachers already are reflective, while others require interventions to promote reflection.

Direct intervention like that recommended by Theis-Sprinthall is one apparently successful means toward developing reflective teachers. Other equally fascinating approaches have been tried. Carl Glickman, for example, has offered a model which categorizes teachers on the basis of cognitive development level (high and low) and on the highly important level of motivation (high and low). Four primary categories of teachers are thus identified for planning appropriate staff development and supervision activities. Tikunoff, Ward and Griffin in 1975 and Griffin, Lieberman, and Noto in 1982 have described programs where teachers become collaborators in research projects, working with professional researchers to examine questions of real importance to them in their daily work. When carefully developed, the research programs offer teachers new roles and careful discussion in the kind of challenging, supportive environment that Thies-Sprinthall concluded was necessary for adult development. So, too, do the teacher seminars led by Margaret Yonemura in which participating teachers are guided in planning, implementing and then reflecting on ongoing dialogues on teaching that they arrange with a single colleague in their own schools. If approached thoughtfully, curriculum development, supervision of student teachers, and implementation of innovations may all provide opportunities to teachers for the kind of professional growth that makes them vital and stimulating for their students.

We can conclude from this line of inquiry that teachers who are "becoming" are teachers whose thinking is growing increasingly complex; they are self-motivated and supported by others in their reflectiveness. They think productively about what they are doing. They don't worry, they do research and solve problems, trying to understand how learning works and why teaching works. The thirty-year veteran who has continued to develop a reflective capacity will have made it possible to renew enthusiasm for teaching because each new encounter with learners may be seen from a new, slightly different perspective. When each day brings something new, enthusiasm is much easier to generate. The words of a continuing teacher hint at this:

> Even though I can look at this kid and say "I've got another of those dudes," or "I've got another one of those bright kids," or "I've got another one of those mediocre-type kids," something about each of those kids surprises me.

The Teacher as Skilled Artisan

The second line of inquiry that sheds light on the work of teachers is that which explores the continuing development of skills. Instructional skills have been the primary focus of most staff development programs. We have worked, for example, on teaching to an objective, questioning strategies, discussion leadership, drill and practice modes, inquiry and discovery teaching, individualized learning approaches, analyzing learning styles, cooperative learning groups, and so forth. We have trained teachers in using these skills because we believed they were linked to different kinds of learning outcomes for students.

Fads in instructional strategies have filled educational journals and taken hours of teachers' inservice training time. Some of the strategies have been confirmed to produce the learning we believed they would; others still await judgment. A relatively coherent research base has begun to develop on "teacher effectiveness," that is, on the skills that make some teachers help students fare better on academic achievement tests. These "effective teacher behavior variables" include task analysis, timing, pacing, praise, and guided practice. N. L. Gage's *The Scientific Basis of the Art of Teaching,* and the chapter by Jere Brophy and Thomas Good in the *Handbook of Research on Teaching* edited by Merlin Wittrock review these ideas cogently.

These teacher behavior patterns not only have been related consistently to higher student academic achievement, we also have been able to teach teachers to *use* these behavior patterns more frequently in their teaching. They are not, in other words, behaviors that some just naturally have, while others never will. Thomas Good and Douglas Grouws found that teachers will begin to use some of these patterns in their classrooms with little outside intervention. For example, many teachers who were given a simple listing of actions that had been found effective in improving students' mathematics test scores began implementing those actions with no additional training or incentives. In the case of more complex instructional techniques, there is evidence that, if teachers are taught how to do them, then given follow-up coaching as they try them out in their everyday work, they will come to incorporate the techniques in their teaching.

Compelling as the work on direct instruction and academic achievement may be, teachers (and those who work with them) must be reminded that achievement test scores measure only one of the several learning outcomes toward which they teach; they must also teach for cognitive development, to enhance individual creativity, and to increase social responsibility. Teaching to these and other important goals requires the artful combination of many strategies, not just those with a strong research base.

Skilled instruction—technical competence—must always be judged in light of the ends to which it is used. The link here is *teacher decision-making*. The instant a teacher decides to use an instructional strategy, she brings together past reflection and technical competence. The quality of decision-making thus depends on the quality of a repertoire of skilled action. A teacher may well know that what ought to be used is a Socratic approach, but will only employ it if he has the technical expertise to do so. On the other hand, he may know perfectly well how to use role playing, but have not the slightest conception of when it is theoretically sound to do so. The ideal is, of course, when he has a deep understanding of and commitment to what ought to occur, and a repertoire of skills from which to select.

N. L. Gage has declared that teaching is an art, albeit an instrumental or practical one. He says that:

> It requires improvisation, spontaneity, the handling of a vast array of considerations of form, style, pace, rhythm, and appropriateness in ways so complex that even computers must lose the way. . . (p. 15)

Teaching is not reducible to systematic formulas, but Gage believes that it nevertheless can have a scientific basis. By this he means that the intentional decisions of individual teachers can and should be informed by the results of research on effective teaching practices.

The early work of researchers in interactive teacher decision-making showed that even though teachers gain experience, many of them use a relatively limited number of predetermined routines to achieve their visualized outcomes. Only when things begin to go wrong—when the image is not being realized—do they look for an alternative. But even then it is likely to be one of a small number of "sub-routines."

Walter Parker and I have described these routinized teachers. But we also drew a picture of the rarer teacher-artist who, though still reliant on routines, seems to hold a larger repertoire of them in mind and hence has far greater flexibility to respond to what is really happening in the classroom. There is evidence from Parker's work that this skill of repertoire development can be taught by providing teachers with opportunities to reflect with their colleagues on their practice.

The Teacher as Whole Person

The last inquiry theme is that of teacher as whole person. It is the broadest of the themes because it attempts to understand teachers, not just as teachers, but as adults who happen to work as teachers. In this research we are looking for elements of teachers' lives in and beyond the classroom which support their continued growth as professionals. Four concepts emerge as particularly important: balance, support, authenticity and connectedness.

Balance. A mature, healthy, growing individual is one who is able to find a balance between the several life roles that must be played: spouse, parent, friend, worker, and so on. "Balance" is, in fact, the term teachers use frequently to describe what they seek in their personal and professional lives. They want to do a good job of teaching, but they also want to be able to enjoy and respond to the needs of their families and friends, engage in hobbies, community activities, and sometimes political action. The nature of teaching makes this difficult. As one very committed teacher said:

> *I think I was realistic about knowing that papers had to be graded and everything, because my mother used to sit around doing them. But still, just thinking about teaching, thinking about the discipline problems, about something someone said, and about going to the ball game, . . . it's just a constant life that is hard to separate. What you have to do is fit your family into that, really.*

To the teachers I studied in their first five years of teaching, the symbol of the balance they sought was an empty-handed exit from school at the end of the day. They envisioned going home without a briefcase full of papers to be corrected; balance was separating school and home.

For most good teachers, this unburdened exit will rarely come true. Goodlad reported in *A Study of Schooling* that 40 percent of the high school teachers claimed to spend 2-3 hours per week per class in preparation and correcting papers; another third spent 4-6 hours per week per class. Though elementary teachers reported somewhat shorter work weeks, they also spent a good portion of the week preparing and grading. That time is very frequently put in while working at home. For women it gets tucked in among other family chores. Any balance of roles comes through skillful interweaving rather than separation. (This interweaving is also the case in the lives of other professionals.)

Until the recent era, teachers' personal lives were dominated by their professional lives through more than just time demands. Joseph Blase and Edward Pajak pointed out that well into the

1930's "little real distinction between a teacher's personal life and professional life existed . . . . His or her private life was actually a public exhibition, fair game for the prying eyes and narrow minds of the local community" (p. 40).

Though such a public life was typical, teachers in some areas of the country experienced considerable opportunities to interweave their roles for their own benefit. Margaret Nelson, in a fascinating study based on interviews with 35 women who had taught in rural Vermont from 1915 to 1950, found that teaching provided a solution to the double burden [home and career]—a solution she believes is nearly unavailable to women today. She described how the women took their small children to school with them rather than try to find daycare, and how they turned their jobs over to friends or relatives during sick leaves or maternity leaves, thus enabling them to return to their jobs when ready.

These Vermont teachers combined work and home responsibilities because they taught during a severe teacher shortage. Rural communities were willing to accommodate them because they were so desperately needed. Things have not been so easy for other teachers, especially those of the 70's and early 80's. Blase and Pajak concluded that today's teachers have gained increased freedom in life-style, but along with it have come increased demands on time and emotional energy. The demands of teaching have carved out resources the teacher might otherwise devote to personal pursuits, or family, social, and community life.

With a predicted teacher shortage in the next few years, teachers may find communities more willing to help them combine their work and personal lives as the rural Vermont teachers once did. Those school districts that have liberal maternity leave policies, job sharing and other part time teaching arrangements, as well as reducing the number of different preparations for teachers, have seen real payoffs. Teachers who feel that their work is a manageable part of a satisfying complete life show that satisfaction in their approach to teaching.

Support. The intrusion of school work in home life is highly visible to family members. If they are not supportive of the teacher's work, they can undermine her personal and professional growth. Dee Ann Spencer-Hall found that some women teachers' husbands did not wish their wives to bring their work home. And, though they themselves worked at night or on weekends, and

went with friends on outings, they wanted their wives to devote
their home time to housework, to children, or to the needs of the
husbands. (Teachers, of course, are not the only women employed
outside the home who experience this dual standard for behavior.)
On the other hand, teachers in Blase and Pajak's study frequently
claimed that among the positive effects of their private lives on
their school lives was the fact that family members gave them
support and stability. One teacher in their study said:

> *My husband gives me 100 percent support with*
> *household or community relationships. I feel as though*
> *I'm on task and don't feel pressured by my job. (p. 28)*

Because teachers are so often isolated from other teachers,
they often must depend on their spouses for counsel. Being able to
go home and tell someone about successes, however small, and
problems, however insignificant, can make teaching less lonely.
And in talking about their experiences, they are engaging, at least
to some degree, in the reflection necessary for improved practice.
To teachers, lack of support and the silence it brings are a straight-
jacket which constricts their growth; support and free exchange
are a wellspring of renewal.

Teachers need support from family and friends, but there may
be little we can do to increase support from these sources. We can,
however, help to ensure a support system among teaching
colleagues. If staff development resources are allocated not just to
improve technical skills but also to encourage more personal
dialogue among teachers, as Arthur Jersild did, we may relieve
family and friends of their overwhelming burden of support.
Perhaps if family members and friends are not called on as the
only listeners, they can be better listeners.

Authenticity and connectedness. The last cluster of factors
from the research on teachers as persons includes authenticity and
connectedness. These are found in the great teachers in literature,
and in the mentors so many seek today. Authentic teachers are, as
Clark Moustakas explained, "teachers who live by truth and value
and love and not by the textbook and by the clock."

Moustakas wrote at length about the strivings toward
authenticity of a group of elementary and secondary teachers with

whom he met in the early 1960's. He concluded that being authentic meant being open and accepting of one's own inner life as a person, being aware of human values as well as intellectual and social values, letting other people be themselves, being open to all experiences and participating in each experience as a new venture. Authenticity develops over time, with much reflection. Authenticity is particularly critical if one believes that the teacher's self is the most important tool in the education of others. One particularly eloquent, authentic teacher quoted by Sara Lawrence Lightfoot concluded that, after better than ten years in the classroom:

> *The most liberating stage of my career was when I could allow not only my students, but also myself to be a whole person in the classroom . . . My teacher-personality and my private-personality finally merged. I no longer felt the strain of "keeping up appearances" in a classroom. Part of this, of course, is just the result of aging—one becomes more comfortable with oneself . . . .*
> *At age thirty-five I do not need to prove to students that I am an adult, and I am not conscious of needing to prove my dominance. (1984, p. 255)*

Connectedness, too, comes with maturity, not just with the passage of time. It is the sense of being linked to others and to something greater than oneself. For example, one of the teachers in the study by Blase and Pajak said:

> *One aspect of my personal life which impacts my career has to do with my spiritual belief that all of us on earth are related and responsible for supporting each other's growth. (p. 35)*

That sense of connectedness deepens and becomes more complex with experience and reflection on the world and one's life meaning within it. If life is small, with little diversity of experience, there is less maturation and opportunity for gaining a sense of connectedness.

Connectedness and authenticity in the teacher's person transmit positive attitudes, interests and experiences to students. In addition, Blase and Pajak stated that "if one's personal life becomes more complex, the number of possible dimensions along which personal contact can be estabished increases, and relationships with students and colleagues improve" (p. 43). Teachers whose lives allow rich and varied experiences beyond their work—through family life, travel, hobbies, study and dialogues with many people—are more likely to develop links to the "past, future, and a transcendental order (secular or sacred) that serves as a source of stability and direction" (p. 43).

Helping teachers achieve a sense of personal identity and connectedness is the kind of "personal project" which teacher educators and administrators must support, along with increased technical skill and reflective practice. Sabbatical leaves, summer travel, study projects, book clubs, graduate study, support groups, and all manner of personal pursuits can be encouraged among teachers for the authenticity and connectedness they bring.

Summary

I began this chapter talking about the teacher's need for a sense of humor. I have tried to show some of the major challenges teachers face over their careers, without painting a picture so bleak that no one would give a second glance to the occupation. The fact is that most teachers do cope with the long hours, the isolation, the guilt, and the fragmentation. However, they don't just cope, they express a high rate of overall job satisfaction, according to Chase's survey of over 2000 teachers in 29 states. They are satisfied because there are many continuing rewards in "the immortal profession," not the least of which is knowing that you have made usually small, but sometimes incredibly large differences in the lives of those with whom you have worked.

While some teachers become the narrow-minded, conservative, retrogressive personalities Willard Waller claimed were typical of teachers in 1932, there are many others "whom teaching liberates" (p. 383), though Waller claimed these persons were rare. The latter half of this chapter has been an attempt to find those factors that would assure professionally liberating careers for more teachers. The inquiry theme of the *reflective practitioner* shows us the need to provide teachers with ample opportunities to pause and think about their own teaching, the goals of education, and their own roles in the scheme. The *artisan* theme shows us the skills, especially decision-making skills, that teachers must continue to perfect. Finally the *teacher as whole person* theme reminds us of the need to help teachers interweave their work with the other aspects of a full life; to help teachers gain the support they need from family, friends, and colleagues; and to assist them as they seek authenticity and connectedness in their lives.

We do not know all there is to know about the teaching career, and we cannot begin to tell all that we already know. We can, however, begin to use what we know to assure that when today's teachers look back after thirty year careers in teaching, they can do so with the firm belief that teaching has been good to them, has served to help them reach their own goals, and has helped them in their own search for meaning, even as they have helped others.

Selected References

Blase, J. J. & E. F. Pajak. A Qualitative Study of the Interaction Between Teachers' Personal and Professional Lives. A paper presented at the annual meeting of the American Educational Research Association. Chicago, Illinois. 1985.

Brophy, J. E. & T. L. Good. Teacher Behavior and Student Achievement. In Merlin Wittrock (Ed.) *Handbook of Research on Teaching.* New York: Macmillan, 1986, 328-375.

Burden, Paul. Teachers' Perceptions of Their Personal and Professional Development. A paper presented at the annual meeting of the Midwestern Educational Research Association. Des Moines, Iowa. November, 1981.

Chase, C. Two Thousand Teachers View Their Profession. *Journal of Educational Research.* 78 (3) January/February, 1985. 12-18.

Cruickshank, D. Uses and Benefits of Reflective Teaching. *Phi Delta Kappan.* 66 (10) June, 1985. 704-706.

Cypher, T. and D. Willower. The Work Behavior of Secondary School Teachers. *Journal of Research and Development in Education.* 18 (1), 1984. 17-24.

Dewey, J. *How We Think: A Restatement of the Relation of Reflective Thinking to the Educative Process.* Chicago: Henry Regnery, 1933.

Feiman-Nemser, S. & R. E. Floden. The Cultures of Teaching. In M. Wittrock (Ed.) *Handbook of Research on Teaching.* New York: Macmillan, 1986. 505-526.

Fuller, F. F. Concerns of Teachers: A Developmental Conceptualization. *American Educational Research Journal.* 6, 1969. 207-226.

Gage, N. L. *The Scientific Basis of the Art of Teaching.* New York: Teachers College Press, 1978.

Glickman, C. *Developmental Supervision.* Alexandria, Virginia: Association for Supervision and Curriculum Development, 1981.

Good, T. & D. Grouws, The Missouri Mathematics Effectiveness Project: An Exploratory Study in Fourth Grade Classrooms. *Journal of Educational Psychology.* 71, 1979. 355-362.

Goodlad, J. I. *A Place Called School: Prospects for the Future.* New York: McGraw-Hill, 1984.

Goodman, J. Reflection and Teacher Education: A Case Study and Theoretical Analysis. *Interchange.* 15 (3), 1984. 9-26.

Greenfield, W. Career Dynamics of Educators: Research and Policy Issues. A paper presented at the Annual Meeting of the American Educational Research Association. New York. March, 1982.

Griffin, G., A. Lieberman, & J. J. Noto. *Interactive Research and Development on Schooling, Final Report of the Implementation of the Strategy.* New York: Teachers College, Columbia University, 1982.

Hall, G. E. & S. Loucks. Teacher Concerns as a Basis for Facilitating and Personalizing Staff Development. In A. Lieberman and L. Miller (Eds.) *Staff Development: New Demands, New Realities, New Perspectives.* New York: Teachers College Press, 1979.

Hunt, D. *Matching Models in Education: The Coordination of Teaching Methods with Student Characteristics.* Toronto: Ontario Institute for Studies in Education, 1971.

Jackson, P. *Life in Classrooms.* New York: Holt, Rinehart & Winston, 1968.

Jersild, A. T. *When Teachers Face Themselves.* New York: Teachers College Press, 1955.

Joyce, B. & B. Showers. Transfer of training: The Contribution of Coaching. *Journal of Education* (1983). 163-172.

Kounin, J. *Discipline and Group Management in Classrooms.* New York: Holt, Rinehart & Winston, 1970.

Kanter, R. *Men and Women of the Corporation.* New York: Basic Books, 1977.

Lieberman, A. & L. Miller. *Teachers, Their World and Their Work: Implications for School Improvement.* Alexandria, Virginia: Association for Supervision and Curriculum Development, 1985.

Lightfoot, S. L. The Lives of Teachers. In L. Shulman and G. Sykes (Eds.) *Handbook of Teaching and Policy.* New York: Longman, 1983. 241-260.

McKibbin, M. & B. Joyce. Psychological States and Staff Development. *Theory into Practice.* 19, 1981. 248-255.

Moustakas, C. *The Authentic Teacher.* Cambridge, Massachusetts: Howard A. Doyle, 1966.

Nelson, M. K. The Intersection of Home and Work: Rural Vermont Schoolteachers, 1915-1950. A paper presented at the annual meeting of the American Educational Research Association. New York. March, 1982.

Parker, W. C. Developing Teachers' Decision-making. *Journal for Experimental Education.* 52 (4), 1984. 220-226.

Parker, W. C. & N. J. Gehrke. Learning Activities and Teachers' Decision-making: Some Grounded Hypotheses. *American Educational Research Journal* (in press).

Peterson, P. L. & C. M. Clark. Teachers' Reports of Their Cognitive Processes During Teaching. *American Educational Research Journal.* 15, 1978. 417-432.

Rosenholtz, S. J. Effective Schools: Interpreting the Evidence. *American Journal of Education.* May, 1985. 352-387.

Ryan, K. Some Feedback is Better Than Others: Implications of a Study of First Year Teachers for the Follow-up of Teacher Education Graduates. A paper presented at the annual meeting of the American Educational Research Association. San Francisco, California. 1979.

Spencer-Hall, D. A. The Home and School Lives of Women Teachers. *The Elementary School Journal.* 84 (3) January, 1984. pp. 283-298.

Sprinthall, N. & L. Thies-Sprinthall. Educating for Teacher Growth: A Cognitive Developmental Perspective. *Theory into Practice,* 9, 1981. 278-286.

Stratemeyer, F. Issues and Problems in Teacher Education. In R. Cottrell (Ed.) *Teacher Education for a Free People.* Washington, D.C.: American Association of Colleges of Teacher Education, 1956.

Thies-Sprinthall, L. Promoting the Developmental Growth of Supervising Teachers: Theory, Research Programs, and Implications. *Journal of Teacher Education.* 35 (3) May/June, 1984. 53-60.

Tikunoff, W. B. Ward, & G. A. Griffin. *Interactive Research and Development in Teaching Study, Final Report.* San Francisco: Far West Laboratory, 1975.

Waller, W. *The Sociology of Teaching.* New York: Russell and Russell, 1961.

Yinger, R. L. & C. M. Clark. Research on Teacher Thinking. *Curriculum Inquiry.* 7, 1977. 279-305.

Yonemura, M. Teacher Conversations: A Potential Source of Their Own Professional Growth. *Curriculum Inquiry.* 12 (3), 1982.   239-256.

5 LEAVING

Being a classroom teacher, what was eventful to record? I engineered no political event, never led a cause, never marched, never demonstrated; yet I felt I lived every teaching day in the very thick of things, with all the apprehension, anguish, despair, and triumph of being on the firing line of human existence.

George Henry
Milton and I

A nd now it is time to leave. Teachers choose to walk away
from teaching, and, unlike George Henry who taught for
46 years, most do so after only a brief stay. Those who
choose to leave teaching at different points along the career path
have different motives for leaving, perhaps different personality
characteristics. But there are few studies that examine these
differences, and no case studies to present the rich detail of
experiences and observations from those in the process of leaving.
Insights must be pieced together from a variety of sources; many
questions are left unanswered.

We can look at leavers in four major groups based on the
timing of their exit. First are the premature leavers, those who
choose to leave before they even begin. Then there are early
leavers, both the voluntary and the involuntary. There are the
mid-life leavers, and finally there are those who retire after a full
career in teaching. As we consider each group's characteristics, we
must ask what conditions would have had to be different for the
persons in that group to have continued to teach. Further, we must
ask how detrimental to the field of education their loss may be and
whether, in the long run, their retention would have been
beneficial.

Before looking at the different groups, however, there are a
few points about general historical and social trends and about the
nature of leaving teaching that seem important to explore.

Trends in Teaching and Leaving

Gender differences. While more women than men have entered teaching (about 3 to 1), men traditionally have "survived" in the occupation longer. So over the years in any one cohort an increasing percentage of men remained. But this pattern reversed in about 1975 according to a longitudinal study by Jonathan Mark and Barry Anderson. Contradictory evidence from another recent study showed that women still lead men in leaving teaching, so generalizations might best be withheld on who is now more likely to leave. There can be little doubt, however, that teaching, like other formerly female dominated careers, is experiencing the effects of women's changing roles in the work force.

Women's work roles have changed dramatically in the last two decades. More women work outside the home than ever before, even after the birth of children. More women head single parent households. Some women work because they wish to; many work because they must. Women teachers are no exception. For many years teaching was attractive to women because it was a career they could pursue early, they could leave to raise families, and they could return to, if they chose, after their families were grown. This factor meant that many young women could be expected to teach a few years, then leave, even if they were happy in the work. Today their leaving patterns have come to look more like those for men; that is, their leaving is more diffused.

The exit point for men always has been much less clear. It was less likely to be tied to an event like marriage or birth of child, but was instead likely to be attributed to dissatisfaction with aspects of teaching and/or to the attractions of another field. Such dissatisfactions and attractions aren't as likely to occur on a recognizable timeline, but are unique to the individual and the context.

Proportion who leave. One thing is clear from all the surveys of teacher attrition: there have always been many who leave teaching at an early stage. The rate of leaving is not necessarily higher today than it has been. For example, Willard Elsbree reported that in the mid-nineteenth century, about a third of all teachers in Pennsylvania had taught less than a year and another one third had taught one to three years. Less than half intended to follow teaching as a career. According to rather consistent reports over the last three decades, nearly 30 percent of those who began teaching left after only one year in the field. Another 30 percent left by the end of the seventh year; twelve percent more left by the fourteenth year. So less than 25 percent have been likely to complete a full career in teaching. In the 1985 study by Mark and Anderson, the teachers who began teaching in 1972 had the highest rate of survival when compared with teachers from 1969 through 1982. But even that 1972 cohort showed only 38 percent surviving in the tenth year, compared with 32.5% for the 1969 cohort.

So teaching is and probably always has been relatively transient work for most people who enter the field. The reported turnover rate (35% after five years) is higher than in nursing (15%) and lower than in social work (74%), according to Cynthia Benton's 1985 study using the data of the National Longitudinal Study of the Class of 1972. Surprisingly, it is about the same as engineering (39%), and lower than computer science (48%) and accounting (54%).

This is not to say that such a high rate of leaving is not problematic or that it is nothing to worry about. It is, and we should. But it is not a new problem, nor is it peculiar to teaching, as many have imagined.

Leaving made easy. A third general consideration when exploring leaving is the structure of the school year and the way that structure affects leaving. Unlike most occupations, teaching has a *seam*—the school year has a distinct beginning and end, with a two to three month break. All begin work together in September; all end work together in May or June. If one is going to leave teaching, one naturally leaves at the end of the school year. In other occupations, except perhaps professional sports, work goes on all year round; it is seamless. Individuals begin working whenever they are hired. They take their vacations whenever most convenient. They leave when they decide to.

Also unlike most other occupations, teaching is marked by a yearly, required recommitment to the work—signing next year's contract (this, too, is commonly found in sports.) Each year the teacher is faced with a time of conscious choice about staying on or leaving. In other occupations there is seldom a point of required recommitment, a point where the merry-go-round stops to let the riders off. Work simply goes on.

The finality of the end of each school year, and the required recommitment combine to make leaving easier for teachers. They can hand in their grades, pack up their things, and say good-bye to the students without feeling guilty about leaving tasks undone—without disrupting the flow.

Given the rather long-standing patterns of early exit from teaching, and the facilitative context schools provide for leave-taking, let us look at the four categories of leavers.

Premature Leavers

Premature leavers are those who receive certification to teach, but never enter teaching at all. This is no small group. A study done by the Texas Research League in 1984 showed about 30 percent of the 8,500 newly certified persons in that state did not take teaching positions that year. In another study, Emily Feistritzer found that one-third of those newly qualifed to teach in 1979-80 were not teaching in 1981. Most of these people applied for teaching jobs, but 38 percent of this group did not even apply. Ninety percent of those who did not apply reported that they simply did not want to teach.

We can see here a number of those earlier identified as drifters, who entered teacher preparation because they really didn't know what they wanted to do. Also among this group are those who complete teacher education programs because of what is called "the mattress theory," a career option to fall back on if needed. None of these individuals would be likely to express high commitment to a teaching career or persevere in locating a teaching position.

David Chapman conducted an extensive state-wide study in Illinois in which he compared those who were certified but had never taught, those who had taught but left, and those who were still teaching. The study showed that initial commitment to teaching was, in fact, lowest for those who had never taught. They did not differ from the others in grade point average or perceptions of the adequacy of their educational preparation. This group of premature leavers may, then, be one about which we can do little to increase retention. Furthermore, education would not necessarily be well served if those who lack a high level of commitment to teaching were somehow enticed to take teaching positions. Our efforts might better be directed at screening them from teacher preparation programs as early as possible so that scarce resources can be invested in those who are likely to go on to teach and to stay longer in teaching.

Early Leavers

Early leavers include both the voluntary and the involuntary. They probably have differences in characteristics, but again there is a dearth of inquiry. Though the early volunteer leaders probably should be grouped and examined by length of stay, there are few studies that give us finely drawn pictures of any differences. This is true despite the fact that several studies cited earlier have found that an extremely large group of teachers leaves after one year (30%) while another comparably-sized group exits over the next six years. The gravest concern, voiced most recently by Phillip Schlechty and Victor Vance as a result of their studies of North Carolina teachers, is that among these early leavers there is a greater than expected percentage of those who have scored higher on measures of aptitude and achievement. This worrisome finding cannot be examined in isolation, however; it must be weighed in relation to other findings on the characteristics of these early leavers.

The Chapman study, mentioned above in discussion of the premature leavers, reported that those who had left teaching within the first five years expressed a higher degree of initial commitment to teaching than did those who never taught, but a less positive experience in their first position than continuing teachers. One cannot know from these findings what may have contributed to these less positive experiences. We do not know whether the situations were particularly troublesome or whether the teachers themselves were less able to deal with the situations, or both.

Some troublesome elements in the first year experience may well be ameliorated by others in the setting, and they certainly should be. Take this description by one teacher in a study by Milbrey McLaughlin and several graduate students in 1986:

> As a beginning teacher, I taught history and math. I received a set of math books — in February! I never did get history books. Instead, every night I wrote history and mimeographed it. My total supplies that year consisted of chalk.

But some elements in the school situation and within the teachers themselves may be less amenable to change. Chapman, for example, concluded that those leaving teaching were more likely to rate salary as important, while continuing teachers rated recognition of family and friends as important. Further, those leaving teaching were more likely to be single and less likely to be a member of a minority group than those who never taught or those who continued teaching. In a study of over 3000 staff members of the Houston Public Schools, Croft, Caram, and Dworkin found that secondary teachers quit sooner and at higher rates than elementary teachers, as did those without added specialized education training.

Other recent studies have concluded that the higher the teacher's socio-economic background, the more likely the person was to leave teaching. John Gosnell argued that family income and status, though significant, were not as highly correlated with attrition in teaching as was whether the person had engaged in a white-collar work experience prior to entering teaching. In either case, one could argue that these teachers have come to hold teaching in lower regard as an occupation and thus regard their own success in the work as less personally satisfying.

Chapman and Hutcheson have also suggested that those teachers who feel less involvement in the professional aspects of their careers and those who have fewer social ties to others in the school are more likely to leave teaching, just as students are more likely to drop out when they do not feel at home in a school. Similarly, Croft, Caram and Dworkin found that "alienation" was a significant contributor to exit from teaching.

So we find that early leavers from teaching do, on the basis of large sample studies, exhibit some differences from those who remain. Chapman noted that a number of the things that seem to be related to teacher exit are not really under the control of school administrators. Initial commitment, salary, occupational status, and the availability of other attractive jobs often are elements over which administrators have little influence. Administrators can, however, influence the quality of the first teaching experience and the enhancement of social ties among teachers in a school. The beginning teacher assistance programs being implemented, especially those which involve peer support, are positive efforts to wield this influence. Studies of the effects of such programs may lead to more conclusive evidence about the nature and source of the problematic first year experiences reported by those who leave teaching early.

Teacher preparation programs also may have a role to play in increasing retention rates, especially among early leavers. Screening candidates not just for academic competence but also for their commitment to teaching, and encouragement of commitment to teaching may better assure that those who ultimately accept positions will stay. Further, realistic preparation of students for the situations they may encounter can prepare them to better cope during their initial years of teaching.

Those competent beginning teachers who voluntarily leave teaching because of the attraction of salaries and prestige in other white-collar jobs may well be convinced to remain in teaching only if major changes in salary patterns and the professional image of teachers occur. Optimists may argue that such major changes are possible. After all, the medical profession managed to do just that several decades ago. Others could argue that given the massive numbers involved in teaching and this society's attitude toward the education of its youth, such changes are unlikely. In her study, *The Conditions of Teaching*, Emily Feistritzer brought together a vast array of descriptive statistics that seemed to support the optimists' position. She pointed to recently rising salaries for teachers across the nation. On the other hand, she did not find positive changes occurring in the environment in which teachers must carry out their work. Instead, she reminded her readers of the new and difficult demands that will be placed on teachers in the coming years as children from different cultures make up an increasing percentage of the school-age population.

The second group of early leavers, the involuntary leavers, includes two essentially different sub-groups: those untenured teachers who leave because they are judged to have performed unsatisfactorily, and those who are laid off, generally for financial reasons. Teachers who are dismissed are hard to separate from those who simply choose to leave very early, because they often are quietly counseled to resign rather than wait to be given notice of the nonrenewal of their contracts. A beginning physical education teacher who was faced with just this situation explained:

> *Mr. Smith called me to his office for a personal conference and he asked for my resignation. He offered no reason even after I asked. He offered me a copy of a resignation . . . he said if I signed then they would give me a good recommendation, otherwise no. I didn't sign . . . I wanted a list of reasons for my dismissal (Templin, 1986, p. 48).*

The teacher later received an official notice of his dismissal stating that his "contribution to the educational program was not of sufficient quality to merit continuation as a teacher" (Templin's case study showed, however, that the teacher had received satisfactory, even good evaluations of his teaching during the year, but had been involved in a dispute with the head athletic coach to whom he reported).

Any figures that one might examine on dismissal due to adjudged performance shortcomings are likely to underrepresent the actual numbers. Few beginning teachers are likely to follow the path of the teacher above and turn down the offer of a good recommendation in return for quiet resignation. How many might return if they *had* been offered another contract cannot be determined, but we can imagine that many who are counseled out or not offered contracts have decided already that they do not wish to continue.

The greatest shortcoming of these dismissed teachers, according to administrators, is in classroom management. But underneath this label is a complex of potential problems, not a single problem. Nearly every aspect of teaching, if not done well, can contribute to what we call a classroom management problem — a badly planned lesson can result in chaos in the classroom, but so can poor interpersonal skills. It may be that the problem of many of these dismissed beginning teachers is that they not only are novices, but they also show little or no promise that they will become experts even given more experience — they do not seem to learn from experience as do the reflective teachers we met in an earlier chapter.

A second group of involuntary leavers is, perhaps, the most tragic of all the groups. It is composed of teachers who are laid off due to declining enrollment, decreasing funds, or changing staffing needs in the district. Those laid off in such reductions in force are nearly always the beginning teachers, although in times of severe change this group may include veteran teachers with ten to fifteen years of experience. During the latter years of the 1970's and the early 1980's many younger teachers, especially in urban areas, were counted in this group.

Though many of the so-called "riffed" teachers find other teaching positions or are called back to their former positions, a large number leave teaching for other occupations. Leaving, for these teachers, is an understandably painful experience. Interviews show them to be bitter, yet grieved about the loss of contact with students and the work they love. They feel angry about the arbitrariness, as this one teacher explained:

> *There was no consideration of the quality of my*
> *teaching; no consideration of the fact that I was*
> *knocking myself out. It was strictly a matter of*
> *numbers.*

Riffed teachers are unlikely to return to teaching, for they often
have found other challenging, financially rewarding work that
they might otherwise never have tried. One riffed teacher, who
turned the situation to her advantage by seeking a doctoral degree,
claimed she might never have done so had she not been jolted by
the experience.

Those who are called back to teaching positions after being
riffed, sometimes several years in a row, are also greatly affected
by this temporary "leave." The trauma, even when called back,
has lasting effects, nearly all negative. The teachers engage in a
host of negative behaviors such as withdrawal, denial, and
substance abuse. They also reduce their involvement in teaching
activities necessary for quality education. One frequently riffed
woman said:

> *You make no long range plans for what you're going to*
> *do in that school the following year to improve the*
> *quality of your program or your classroom setting.*

Others report less curriculum material development, no bulletin
boards or special displays, late arrival and early departures from
school each day, no extracurricular work or special committees.

Murnane and Phillips have presented evidence that the group
of teachers who entered teaching during the 1970's when teaching
jobs were scarce were among a better "vintage." That is, they were
more able than those who entered earlier. These very teachers
were the ones who were riffed in large numbers. We can recognize
in this group of involuntary leavers, then, a real loss to education
— a loss that, with more careful planning, often could have been
avoided. As we move into a period of teacher shortage, the
traumas of riffing are likely to be forgotten for a time. But
inevitably market demands will again decrease and layoffs will
once again occur. We only can hope that those managing future
situations will have learned something from the past.

Mid-career Leavers

With anywhere from 35 to 60 percent of those who enter teaching leaving by the end of the seventh year, one would expect the committed group that remains longer but leaves before completing a full teaching career to have been far more studied, even far more pampered than they have been. Instead, they seem to have been treated as particularly uninteresting, both in research and in practice. Yet it is this group that may be considered the backbone of any school — the formal and informal leaders — this group from which committee chairs, department chairs, principals, district administrators, and supervisors are drawn.

The results of most of the large studies have been summarized in the section on early leavers because these studies, for various reasons, examined attrition (or retention) primarily in the earlier years. The study of Houston teachers by Croft, Caram, and Dworkin can shed some light on the mid-career leavers, though it does not seek to differentiate teachers by years of experience (in fact, the more senior the teachers the less any large scale study differentiates them, often grouping all teachers with over 20 years of experience together).

The Houston study concluded that two factors directly contributed to teachers' quitting: having appropriate skills to apply in available alternative careers; and role alientation, a combination of powerlessness, meaninglessness, isolation, normlessness, and estrangement. Individuals, then, seem to be both pulled into other careers by opportunities and pushed into other careers by negative factors in teaching. If the investment of self in teaching is high, as represented by years of service and by the acquisition of additional specialized training, then teachers are unlikely to leave, unless they experience severe role alienation.

Alienated teachers should be of concern for two reasons. First, because if they leave they take specialized knowledge with them and leave a diminished program; second, because if they stay and continue to be alienated they will mean diminished effectiveness — retirement on the job. In a report of a study of 1,869 teachers in Southern Ontario, Robert Knoop gave an extensive composite description of alienated teachers. These teachers had taught at the same school for a long period of time, had lower self-esteem, believed they had less autonomy, perceived less feedback from peers and supervisors, saw leaders as less considerate and more structured, participated less in decision-making, and were less satisfied with the supervision received yet felt more closely supervised, were less satisfied with co-workers and with teaching, were less motivated by their own work, and felt more powerless. In this composite picture of alienation we see many of the factors addressed by the studies on teacher growth in the earlier chapter.

Clearly a number of the characteristics of alienated teachers can be altered by changes in the environments in which they work. Some of the current recommendations for changes in the conditions of teaching are directly related to a reduction in the alienation of teachers and, one might hope, the retention of those master teachers who leave at the mid-career point. The proposals include more involvement in decision-making, especially about curriculum, textbooks, and instructional strategies; more teacher interaction; changes in supervision and evaluation; more praise for success and reward for innovations; and greater opportunity for reflection and inquiry.

These widely recommended contemporary proposals are by no means new. A 1970 book on the teacher dropout recommended similar measures. Even earlier, in 1939, Willard Elsbree wrote the following, with a special focus on the need for teacher participation in decision-making:

> The time is rapidly approaching when the old hierarchy which placed the teacher in a position subservient to that occupied by principals, supervisors, and administrators will disappear. A division of labor will be maintained, but the freedom of the professional teacher to pursue her work without interference will constitute the crowning achievement of a long chapter in the history of the profession.

It does seem strange that though educators have been well aware of the need for changes in the conditions of teaching for fifty years, those conditions apparently have not changed sufficiently to stem the constant loss of teachers from the profession. Hear the words of one middle-school teacher:

> Things are set up these days so that teachers never feel they can do a good job. The classes are too large, the materials aren't there, and the students come to school with incredible needs that teachers can't meet. We are constantly pushed. We are constantly told by the superintendent that teachers have to do this, and we are

> *constantly told by parents that teachers have to do that.
> . . . I feel angry; I feel depressed; I feel frustrated. It is a
> very difficult situation for those teachers who care.
> (McLaughlin, Pfeifer, Swanson-Owen, & Yee, 1986, p.
> 421)*

And many believe that the mid-career leavers are, in fact, the
teachers who care and who are especially talented. Mary Ellen
Grimes, a psychotherapist and former teacher and school
counselor in Seattle, does outplacement counseling with teachers
contemplating mid-career changes. She is convinced that those
who leave are "the best." Grimes sees at least two major groups of
mid-career leavers: those who are dedicated, frustrated people,
who have been told "Be perfect; be strong; do it all;" and those
who, at mid-career, feel the need for a new challenge and say, "I
loved it, but now it's time to do something else."

An important point in all of this is that the teachers rarely
point to money as the driving force in their exit from teaching.
They do raise the issue of low salary, but salary alone is almost
never heard as the single compelling cause of exit for mid-career
leavers. In many cases the low salary comes to be among the
issues, not just because it means a strained financial existence, but
because of what it symbolizes—the low esteem in which the
community holds the teacher's efforts (remember, that those who
enter service occupations do so because of intrinsic rewards, and
are more affected by the praise and support of family and friends
than are those who choose other kinds of occupations.)

That is why Susan Rosenholtz among others predicts that, if
the only thing to change in current efforts to upgrade the teaching
profession is the salary, we may attract more competent people,
but their eventual loss will not be stemmed. Without the
concurrent implementation of policies that reduce the isolation of
teachers, change leadership and decision-making patterns,
increase teacher collaboration through group incentives, alter the
nature of supervision and evaluation, and provide support and
praise for jobs well done, higher pay will produce few changes in
teacher retention patterns *or* improved educational programs for
youth.

An aside must be made here about attracting one-time
teachers back into the profession. Though we hear much about
this re-entry concept as a response to the coming teacher shortage,
there is little reason to be optimistic. The 1985 Metropolitan Life

Survey of Former Teachers reported that an overwhelming majority (83%) of ex-teachers surveyed say they have found higher salaries and greater job satisfaction and are unlikely to return to teaching. The sample for this large survey (500) was by no means representative, however, for 2 out of 3 were men, and 7 of 10 had taught high school. Being cautious in interpretation of the results, we can still benefit from heeding one of the study's conclusions:

> *Policy-makers ought not pin their main hopes on any big increase in the return rate of those who have already left . . . . If we wish to retain the teachers we have, we should concentrate on doing so before they leave, rather than hoping to attract them back after they have walked out the door and taken new jobs.*

Career Teachers and Retirement

So we come, finally, to that small, elite group of individuals who make teaching a full life career. Though our first tendency when thinking about career-teachers is to place them in the company of saints, they too come in a wide variety. Some are indeed saintly, others are curmudgeons; some are youthful and lively, others are fragile and tired. They have in common years of work with thousands of young students, unending chalk-white and ditto-blue fingertips, an infinity of lesson plans and paper grading, and a growing awareness of younger and younger colleagues and principals.

They have reached the career stage Bernice Neugarten labels disengagement; others call it wind-down. They are, judging from the dearth of research, generally ignored, tolerated or undifferentiated from other teachers until the very day of retirement. Then they are feted briefly, as retirees usually are. Unless their performance falls to a level that provokes the anger of parents and thus the principal's effort to counsel early retirement, senior teachers just keep on keeping on. Some become legends; most remain anonymous to all but their students and fellow teachers.

But their leaving is unlike that of the earlier leavers. While the younger teachers who exit often hold private the knowledge that they are contemplating leaving, the career teacher's retirement is usually a surprise to no one. It is likely to be discussed quite openly, if not frequently, by the teacher and by colleagues. This discussion can uncover great anxiety or great anticipation about the post-retirement era, and a great sadness or great joy at bringing closure to a career. In one of the few studies of the lives of older teachers, Katherine Newman found that many spent a considerable amount of effort deciding whether to retire. Some wished to retire but could not afford it. Some were looking forward to the opportunity to attend to hobbies and other interests. Some looked back on good careers but were beginning to feel exhausted and ready to step out. One tired teacher in Newman's study said:

> When I started teaching, I had six classes with about forty-three in each class. If I had not been young I could not have handled it. Today I have only twenty-seven in each class and only five classes, and I am shot by the end of the day. So the load is about half, but the kids are so different that it takes every bit of energy to keep them in line, keep them going and keep them responding. I've enjoyed teaching up to this point. I'm really tired this year.

Late adulthood (from approximately 55 on) is a period in life marked by a continuity of personal outlook, gradually declining energy, and psychological and social disengagement—a kind of drawing inside oneself. If this period is common for most in late adulthood, we should not be surprised to find it true for teachers. It does help us interpret the findings of David Ryans that teachers who were 55 or older claimed they were less friendly and understanding and liked students less than did younger teachers. Anne Peterson has suggested that this process of disengagement has a functional value because:

> the aging person prepares to set aside certain respon-
> sibilities at the same time that society no longer needs or
> wants his active social involvement. (1979, p. 9).
> 9).

Thus it may be that the combined decline in energy and the increasing inward orientation of aging teachers begin to prepare them to leave their life-long career with young people.

Peterson's interviews with fifty retired secondary teachers who had an average of over 38 years in the classroom showed that, as the teachers had neared retirement, they had experienced a lessening in their commitment to teaching that seemed to be linked with a decrease in energy. This late decline in commitment to teaching often was accompanied by a perception of a negative change in some element of the school environment—a change in the students or the school, a change in academic standards or in colleagues. In keeping with earlier research, the retired teachers most frequently pinpointed this negative change as occurring when they were about 55, regardless of historical circumstances or length of time until actual retirement.

Half of the interviewed teachers, however, indicated that their happiest time in teaching had occurred between the ages of forty-five and sixty. This may come as somewhat of a surprise, but also as a reassurance that teaching can still provide much satisfaction in the latter years of a full career. Fully two-thirds of the teachers interviewed said that they had retired from teaching feeling satisfied with themselves and their careers. As one man put it, "Teaching helped my life to be a full life. Life wouldn't have been as full in other areas."

An unspecified number of these satisfied teachers claimed to regret having to retire and only left because they had reached the mandatory age of retirement. One man said: "I never worked a day in my life. I had fun." Peterson concluded that teachers in the era from 55 to retirement were generally able to maintain high job morale, even though they sensed that their most productive and fulfilling years in teaching were behind them.

We are faced with a dilemma when we consider retiring career teachers as a group. With those who have lost the energy, interest, and joy in their work, a mandatory retirement age seems very attractive. On the other hand those who can continue to bring a zest for living and learning to their work would be wonderful to retain as long as they wished to stay. How much would have been lost if, for example, Ruth Elster had not become a nearly full-time substitute teacher after she "retired" from teaching. Writing of her substitute work, she said:

> I seldom refuse a call. Like the old fire horse, when that early bell rings, in no time at all I'm up and away, sometimes at minus 30 temperature, with my well-worn Mexican bag bulging with "something interesting."
> (1972, p. 419)

Or take the words of Herbert von Roeder, who had taken five different successive teaching and administrative jobs after retiring first at age 66:

> *I do not think a person should ever completely retire as long as he can contribute something to society. . . . I had promised my wife I would retire for good at age 75; however, I am now 81 years of age and have been employed for some time as director of an institute for lifelong learning for senior citizens. As soon as the institute finds someone to replace me, I plan to "retire" again. (1976, p. 649)*

Such youthful exuberance about being part of the educational scene, being useful to society, makes clear that a lifetime in teaching need not result in a reduced capacity to engage in shaping the lives of others. Those masters nearing retirement, and their potential students, might well benefit from the artful creation of emeritus teaching roles like those of college professors. Such roles may be more limited in scope and energy demands, but no less challenging and interesting than traditional teaching positions. Emeritus teaching positions could allow people to continue to practice the profession they love, yet give them the freedom to pursue other interests as well.

If the creative tailoring of roles for master teachers at the wind down phase of their careers is a sound educational idea, the tailoring of roles for good teachers at other points in their careers is equally sound. If we make changes in the teacher role that adjust it to the individual's needs, rather than forcing the individual to conform totally to an inflexibly defined role, we may just see more teachers completing full careers, rather than leaving at mid-career or earlier.

We should seek to assure that all teachers look back to see their first choice to teach and each successive year's recommitment as good decisions. They should all have constant opportunities to grow as professionals and as human beings. They should all know how much we value their contributions to future generations—value them as vital links between past and future. They should all look back with deep satisfaction on the lives they spent "on the firing line of human existence."

Selected References

Benton, C. Predicting occupational persistence: A comparison of teachers and five other occupational groups. A paper presented at the annual meeting of the American Educational Research Association. Chicago, Illinois. 1985.

Bloland, P. A. and T. Selby. Factors associated with career change among secondary school teachers: A review of the literature. *Educational Research Quarterly*. 5 (3), 1980. 13-24.

Bogad, C. Recruitment and socialization as recurring issues in teacher education. A paper presented at the annual meeting of the American Educational Research Association. New Orleans, Louisiana. 1984.

Burke, P. J., J. C. Christensen, and R. Fessler. *Teacher career stages: Implications for staff development*. Bloomington, Indiana: Phi Delta Kappa, 1984.

Chapman, D. W. and S. M. Hutcheson. Attrition from teaching careers: A discriminant analysis. *American Educational Research Journal*. 21(3), 1984. 645-658.

Charters, W. W., Jr. Some factors affecting teacher survival rates in school districts. *American Educational Research Journal*. 7(1), 1970. 1-27.

Corrigan, D. Politics and educational reform. *Journal of Teacher Education*. 36(1), 1985. 8-11.

Croft, J. C., D. F. Caram, and A. G. Dworkin. Some relationships between administrators' opinions and teachers' quitting behavior in urban public school systems. A paper presented at the annual meeting of the American Educational Research Association. Montreal, Canada. 1983.

Elsbree, W. S. *The American teacher*. New York: American Book Company, 1939.

Elster, R. Looking back with appreciation. *Childhood Education*. 48(8), 1972. 416-420.

Feistritzer, C. E. *The conditions of teaching: A state by state analysis*. Princeton, New Jersey: Carnegie Foundation for the Advancement of Teaching, 1985.

Gehrke, N. J. and R. Sheffield. Career mobility of women and minority high school teachers during decline. *Journal of Research and Development in Education*. 18(4), 1985. 39-49.

Gehrke, N. J. and H. K. Taylor. Teacher socialization through professional crises. A paper presented at the annual meeting of the American Educational Research Association. San Francisco, California. 1986.

Gosnell, J. The relationship between work experience and occupational aspirations and attrition from teaching. *The Clearinghouse*. 51, 1977. 176-179.

Grimes, M. E. Remarks from an interview. October, 1985.

Henry, G. H. Milton and I: Teaching English in paradise re-lost. *English Journal*, 64(8), 1975. 32-38.

Knoop, R. The alienated teacher. A paper presented at the annual meeting of the American Educational Research Association. New York, New York. 1982.

Mar, J. and B. D. Anderson. Teacher survival rates in St. Louis, 1969-1982. *American Educational Research Journal*. 22(3),1985. 413-421.

McLauglin, M., R. S. Pfeifer, D. Swanson-Owen, and S. Yee. Why teachers won't teach. *Phi Delta Kappan*. 67(6), 1986. 420-426.

Metropolitan Life Insurance Company. *Survey of former teachers*. New York, N.Y.: Metropolitan Life Insurance Company, 1985.

Murnane, R. J. and B. R. Phillips. Learning by doing, vintage, and selection: Three pieces of the puzzle relating teaching experience and teaching performance. *Economics of Education Review*. 1(4), 1981. 453-466.

Neugarten, B. L. *Middle-age and aging*. Chicago, Illinois: University of Chicago Press, 1968.

Newman, K. Middle-aged experienced teachers' perceptions of their career development. A paper presented at the annual meeting of the American Educational Research Association. San Francisco, California. 1979.

Pavalko, R. M. Recruitment to teaching: Patterns of selection and retention. *Sociology of Education*. 43, Summer 1970. 340-353.

Peterson, A. R. Teachers' changing perceptions of self and others throughout the teaching career: Some perspectives from an interview study of 50 retired secondary school teachers. A paper presented at the annual meeting of the American Educational Research Association. San Francisco, California. 1979.

Rosenholtz, S. J. Political myths about education reform: Lessons from research on teaching. *Phi Delta Kappan*. 66(5), 1985.349-355.

Schlechty, P. C. and V. S. Vance. Do academically able teachers leave education? The North Carolina case. *Phi Delta Kappan*. 63(1), 1981. 106-112.

Templin, Thomas. Taking on Goliath. *Journal of Physical Education, Recreation and Dance*. 57(4), 1986. 47-49.

Von Roeder, H. Excerpts from an octogenarian's letter. *Phi Delta Kappan*. 57 (10), 1976. 649.

Whitener, J. E. An actuarial approach to teacher turnover. Unpublished doctoral dissertation. Washington University, St. Louis, Missouri, 1965.

EPILOGUE

Let it be said of us
that we worked diligently to teach;
That our example gave strength
to the children.
That our inspiration will be a part
of each life that we touched.

Elsie Evans
Epitaph for the Educator

I began this work with the beliefs that teaching is a tendency of all human beings, that it is a worthy career, a profession requiring reflection, and an opportunity to become more fully human — to find one's being. Having completed the work of the five main chapters, I hold those beliefs even more strongly. And now I bring this exploration of teaching to a close. After all the months of combing the literature, looking for patterns, seeking exemplary remarks and cases, writing and rewriting, I am nearly at a loss for something more to add. After all these words, what can one person say to truly deepen another's understanding of what it means to spend one's life in teaching?

Yet I know, in a practical sense, that there is more to say, because there are many questions yet unanswered. And, though I've tried to be thorough, I have unquestionably missed important contributions. Moreover, each day brings additional books and articles that report on previously ignored or unrecognized facets of teaching.

Of course, one could argue that much of what appears today on the topic of teaching is redundant or wrong-headed. While there may well be useless material in print, I believe there are writings that offer bits of wisdom too. The experience of writing each chapter here has confirmed that belief. It also confirmed the belief that researchers need to use many different modes of inquiry to expand our understanding of this "basic human tendency." Standing back *and* getting close are both required for understanding teaching as life and work.

Choosing teaching. More than ever I am convinced that those of us who have chosen teaching — with preschoolers, elementary school children, adolescents, or adults — have chosen a way of life that offers more opportunities for satisfaction than most. True, the financial rewards are far from great, but the personal rewards can be bountiful. Who can explain, except in a superficial way, about the satisfactions to be gained from this work? About the sense of being part of something greater than oneself when one commits to teaching the next generation — the connectedness that teaching can bring? About the many invaluable "gifts" that one receives during a teaching career? These gifts may or may not be what made many of us choose teaching the first time, but they are high on the lists of those who renew that choice year after year. Walt Whitman once said: "The gift is to the giver and comes back most to him." Teachers well understand what he meant.

Learning to teach. In continuing to learn about teaching throughout our careers we are, in fact, continuing to make ourselves more human. It isn't just teaching that makes one more human; it is the focus on *learning* about teaching, thinking about teaching, hence thinking about thinking — turning consciousness in on itself that makes for growth. This growth is characterized not only by richer conceptions of reality, but also by deeper understandings of what it means to strive for the humane life.

Not everyone who adopts the role of teacher will seize the opportunity to use it toward becoming more human. But if teacher education and staff development efforts focused a bit more on the goals of understanding and reflection rather than on the perfection of teachers' instructional skills, we might find far better results in teacher growth and student growth than we now can claim.

Beginnings in teaching. In a way, if we continue to learn to teach throughout our careers, we are always beginners. If real learning implies posing new problems for ourselves, trying out something we haven't done before, and then thinking about the results, then even experienced, reflective teachers are beginning again all the time. This learning is one of the good parts that too many people are forgetting right now as they surge zealously to solve "the problem of the beginning teacher." In an effort to be helpful, we may just be overstating the problematic nature of being a beginner, creating more rather than less anxiety. There are, after all, good things about beginning. Beginning brings challenges, demands our full effort, and is therefore exhilarating. Each success is a first, and firsts are satisfying. They prove to us that we are competent people.

The anxiety of being a first-year teacher is and should be assuaged both by supportive programs and by years of experience. But the good elements of being a beginner must be celebrated with beginners; they must also be sustained by the continuing teacher. Again, staff development can play an important role in welcoming *and* sustaining the vitality of beginning through a focus on learning about teaching.

Continuing to teach. Teaching is not without its obvious problems, whether one is just beginning, continuing, or nearing retirement. But many of these problems are not peculiar to teaching. Many that are, are solvable. When educators and the public seriously turn their attention to such problems as beginners' trauma, or experienced teachers' stagnation, or the isolation experienced by teachers at all stages, the problems can and do give way. We find evidence that there are workable responses to the challenges of renewing enthusiasm and sustaining growth throughout the middle and latter years of a teaching career. Given the opportunity, teachers themselves, working with support staff, administrators, and college educators, have generated an array of alternative strategies for enhancing their own personal and professional growth — being alive in and through teaching. They also have found ways of being with each other, listening to each other, collaborating — being friends. They can counter the isolation often brought by their work.

Because some teachers have solved the problems common to their occupation does not mean that most have. Many teachers still live with those problems on a daily basis. But just knowing that some have dealt with the difficulties (and not by leaving the field) lends optimism to efforts to help others as they continue to seek satisfaction through teaching.

Leaving teaching. Teachers leave teaching at many different times and for many different reasons. Some complete full careers, others leave after only a few years, and still others leave before they've ever actually begun. Some leave because of problems within the work environment or problems in their preparation or selection; others leave because of personal goals or unique needs. Our greatest concern must be for those who leave early because of problems in the occupation or in the school environment — problems that we know we can solve, *if* we choose to. Our concern also should be focused on those who leave prematurely, either because of poor educational experiences or because of inappropriate selection processes. These too are problems that can be solved.

But we ought to stop agonizing when some capable individuals decide to move on to other occupations because of personal life goals rather than because of problems within teaching itself. Many people change jobs with regularity, and they often do so because of a need for stimulation — for variety, for new and different challenges. One occupation, however exciting, prestigious, or financially rewarding, can seldom contain all the possible options that all individuals want for themselves. Furthermore, it is likely that, in every occupation, the most capable will be among the first to feel the need for greater variety and subsequently seek change. There is, in other words, probably little we would find unique about the turnover pattern in teaching today, if we would take the time to compare teaching with other occupations.

Though patterns of leaving teaching may not be unique, there may even be some unique social benefits from teacher turnover to which we may have paid too little attention. Those benefits come from the dispersion of former teachers throughout society. If there were any one occupation's skills, values, and interests that we might wish to have distributed across the general population, would it not be those of teaching?

I think so, for several reasons. First, while we as human beings are given the tendency to teach, we can all benefit from increased skills in teaching others and from being surrounded by those who also have increased skills. Teaching goes on in all kinds of work settings, home situations, and community environments; all can benefit from more skilled approaches. Former teachers can bring them.

Second, we all can benefit individually and as a community from strengthening the values that teachers hold: the worth of the individual, the love of learning, the importance of the search for knowledge, the power of cooperation in groups, the greatness of giving. People who leave teaching do not lose all their skills, do not forsake all these critical values, and do not, I would venture, lose their interest in what is happening in the schools and classrooms of which they were once a part.

Without overstating the case, what they embodied as teachers, and continue to exhibit as they pursue other occupations, are some of the essential characteristics of the enlightened citizen. The schools may feel a direct loss when good teachers leave, but they and society in general may well continue to receive both direct and indirect benefits from the continuing participation of these former teachers in the life of the social group. In a way we could say that teachers never really leave teaching, they just change contexts.

Being in teaching. No other occupational group has been as regularly and frequently damned in public (while certain of its individual members are so warmly praised) as teaching has. But then, no other occupational group has been charged with the massive daily contact with "the public" that teachers have. Teaching might be seen as a frontline occupation — one of the most visible — for it goes on in every community and touches nearly everyone either directly or indirectly every day. It is far from the invisible roles that many people play — important roles, no doubt, but nevertheless roles where no one can ever link an individual person to particular outcomes, good or bad.

Being in teaching, then, is a life that only responsible individuals can manage, for every day someone holds them accountable for what they have accomplished. Yet the most significant differences that teachers make are often the slowest in developing, the least easily detected by those who would evaluate them. They are the subtle changes in thinking, attitude, values, or self-esteem that require not just skill, but a full personal investment in students. So teachers must be sensitive and caring, as well as responsive to the frequent demands for quick results. They must also be toughened to the adverse criticism that may arise when they are not fast enough in producing measurable outcomes while they are trying to effect the long-term growth they know their students need. Quick, yet patient; tough, yet sensitive; responsible, yet responsive. Can anyone be all this?

So, of course, being in teaching is difficult. It does bring with it apprehension, anguish, and despair. But it also brings with it the sense of being alive, of knowing "that our legacy is marvelously woven into the fabric of being," as Elsie Evans wrote in closing her tribute to teachers. Would that every career could bring that sense of vibrance to its members!